STUART THOMAS
Christ, Our Peace
Reflective Services for Lent and Holy Week

Kevin Mayhew

First published in 1996 by
KEVIN MAYHEW LTD
Rattlesden
Bury St Edmunds
Suffolk IP30 0SZ

© 1996 Kevin Mayhew Ltd

The right of Stuart Thomas to be identified as the author of this work has been asserted by him in accordance with the Copyright, Designs and Patents Act 1988.

All rights reserved. No part of this publication may be reproduced, stored in a retrieval system, or transmitted, in any form or by any means, electronic, mechanical, photocopying, recording or otherwise, without the prior written permission of the publisher.

0 1 2 3 4 5 6 7 8 9

Scripture quotations taken from the HOLY BIBLE,
NEW INTERNATIONAL VERSION.
Copyright © 1973, 1978, 1984 by International Bible Society.
Used by permission of Hodder & Stoughton Limited.
All rights reserved.

'NIV' is a registered trademark of International Bible Society.
UK trademark number 1448790

ISBN 0 86209 898 X
Catalogue No 1500076

Front cover: *The Resurrection of Christ* by Fra Bartolommeo (1472-1517). Reproduced by courtesy of Palazzo Pitti, Florence/Bridgeman Art Library, London.

Cover design by Veronica Ward and Graham Johnstone
Typesetting by Vicky Brown
Printed and bound in Great Britain.

Contents

Introduction	5
First Sunday in Lent	7
Second Sunday in Lent	11
Third Sunday in Lent	16
Fourth Sunday in Lent	20
Passion Sunday	24
Palm Sunday	28

Introduction

For the early Christians the six weeks leading up to Easter were the time when candidates for baptism were prepared for the step they were about to take. As well as being a time of instruction in the Christian faith, it was also a time for reflection and meditation, prior to starting out on a lifetime of witness and service. Lent still has both of those aims, and this book of short reflective services is directed towards the latter. It recognises that such services may not attract vast congregations, but also rejoices in the presence of the Lord Jesus 'wherever two or three are gathered'. Each service can stand on its own but, equally, the individual elements can be extracted and used in other contexts as appropriate.

The material is based on the ASB readings for each Sunday in Lent and loosely follows the ASB themes, but it is entirely independent and designed to be used by churches or Christian groups of any tradition. The songs are all taken from the New Anglican Edition of *Hymns Old & New* (Kevin Mayhew, 1996). They have been selected to match the themes and reflective nature of the liturgy, but in particular contexts others may be more suitable.

I make no apology for the fairly strong emphasis on our activity as Christians, because however important reflection and meditation are in the Christian tradition, they have little value if they don't result in hearts and lives which are changed by God, through his Spirit, to make a difference to the world. Just as the earliest believers underwent instruction in the faith so that they could then go out and live it (and frequently die for it, too), so we use Lent as a time for self-examination and repentance, in its literal sense of 'rethinking', to become transformed ever more into the likeness of our Saviour and demonstrate his love and power to an increasingly desperate world. If this little book makes a contribution to that aim, it will have fulfilled its purpose.

STUART THOMAS

First Sunday in Lent

Leader   Jesus is our great high priest who has gone into heaven. Let us then approach the throne of grace with confidence, to receive help in time of need.

Silence

Leader   Lord Jesus, eternal King and Lord of all, you emptied yourself of all but love to live as one of us. In every way you were tempted as we are, though without sinning, and sympathise with us in our weakness. As we turn to you now, may we find in your loving presence strength to endure the times of testing, courage to face the conflict with evil, and mercy to restore us when we fall, that as you once shared our human life, so we may share also your eternal life. This we ask in your holy name. Amen.

SONG   *We will lay our burden down* (Iona Community)

Leader   Jesus himself suffered when he was tempted, so he is able to help those who are being tempted. Since we share in the heavenly calling, may we fix our eyes upon him and not turn away from the living God with an unbelieving heart;

All   instead let us encourage one another every day.

Leader   May we not disobey and rebel, hardening our hearts when we hear God's voice;

All   instead let us enter into his promised rest.

Leader   May we not resist his living and active word, which judges the deepest thoughts of our hearts;

All   instead let us hold firmly to the faith we profess.

Leader   May we not forget Jesus, our great high priest, who has gone through the heavens;

All   instead let us approach his throne with confidence, to receive mercy and find grace in our time of need.

8 First Sunday in Lent

READING
Matthew 4:1-11

Jesus was led by the Spirit into the desert to be tempted by the devil. After fasting for forty days and forty nights he was hungry. The tempter came to him and said, 'If you are the Son of God, tell these stones to become bread'. Jesus answered, 'It is written: "Man does not live on bread alone, but on every word that comes from the mouth of God."'

Then the devil took him to the holy city and had him stand on the highest point of the temple. 'If you are the Son of God,' he said, 'throw yourself down. For it is written: "He will command his angels concerning you, and they will lift you up in their hands, so that you will not strike your foot against a stone."' Jesus answered him, 'It is also written: "Do not put the Lord your God to the test."'

Again the devil took him to a very high mountain and showed him all the kingdoms of the world and their splendour. 'All this I will give you,' he said, 'if you will bow down and worship me.' Jesus said to him, 'Away from me, Satan! For it is written: "Worship the Lord your God and serve him only."' Then the devil left him and angels came and attended him.

MEDITATION

The temptations which Jesus endured during his time of prayer and fasting may seem strange at first glance, but a closer look reveals them to be basic to all of us. The first is materialism, which puts the highest priority on things we can touch, see or experience. There's nothing wrong with bread, or anything else which derives from God's creation, but if we allow it to exclude the Creator we will only ever receive nourishment for our human bodies, leaving us to starve spiritually. Ask yourself how important the material world is in your life; how much time do you spend worrying about financial concerns or physical well-being; what priority do you give to your relationship with God? The second is fatalism, which, in its belief that all events are predetermined, takes away human responsibility and blames God for anything that goes wrong. How easy do you find it to accept your ability to influence not only your own but others' circumstances too; how readily do you blame God (or other external forces) rather than facing up to personal accountability? The third is hunger for power, arguably the greatest of all corrupting influences, and not one the Church has always been exempt from. Do you find yourself tempted to manoeuvre into positions from which you can exercise greater control; do you recognise the destructive tendencies of power? Jesus refused to give in to any of these very human temptations, though in his weakened state he must have felt vulnerable. Temptation is usually strongest when we're at our weakest, and we can only resist it, as Jesus did, with the words and authority of God. Ask God for wisdom to recognise temptation, however human it may seem, and for strength to stand firm against its subtle and persistent force.

Leader	We come into the presence of Jesus, who was tempted like us though without sin, saying, Lord, forgive our weakness,
All	and increase our trust in you.
Leader	When we are tempted to put our human interests above your eternal kingdom, Lord, forgive our selfishness,
All	and increase our vision of you.
Leader	When we are tempted to disclaim responsibility rather than confront what is wrong, Lord, forgive our self-interest,
All	and increase our commitment to you.
Leader	When we are tempted to gather power for ourselves instead of proclaiming your glory, Lord, forgive our pride,
All	and increase our love for you.
Leader	When we are tempted to give up on our faith rather than acting on your word, Lord, forgive our apathy,
All	and increase our willingness to serve you without counting the cost, so that your kingdom is able to grow until the whole earth owns you as Lord. Amen.

SONG *Give thanks with a grateful heart* (Henry Smith)

Leader	In silence we ask God for courage to withstand the temptations of our human nature and to uphold his kingdom of righteousness, justice and peace.

Silence

Leader	We pray for those in authority who might be tempted to use power to fulfil selfish ambition rather than to serve you

	selflessly. May they honour you, the source of all authority, and direct their decisions to the good of all. Sovereign Lord, in your mercy,
All	make us humble.
Leader	We pray for the poor and exploited, who might be tempted to resort to wrong actions to escape from their circumstances. May they know you, the faithful friend, and trust you to bring them out of their troubles. Sovereign Lord, in your mercy,
All	make us loyal.
Leader	We pray for those who communicate news and information, who might be tempted to distort the truth or give a misleading impression. May they respect you, the God of all truth, and work to create a society based on honesty and trust. Sovereign Lord, in your mercy,
All	make us truthful.
Leader	We pray for any who feel lonely or despairing, who might be tempted to give up or live only for themselves. May they put their trust in you, the God who heals and restores, and live on this earth in the light of your heavenly calling. Sovereign Lord, in your mercy,
All	make us faithful servants of your kingdom, confident of the love and grace of our Lord Jesus Christ who gives strength to withstand temptation and overcome the forces of evil, so that on the last day we may hear you say 'Well done'. Amen.
All	Our Father . . .
Leader	As we leave this place, may we know the presence of the Lord Jesus in our hearts and lives. In our homes and families,
All	may he come and dwell.
Leader	In our work and leisure,
All	may he give strength and joy.
Leader	In our thoughts and actions,
All	may he direct us in the ways of truth.
Leader	Let us bless the Lord.
All	Thanks be to God.

Second Sunday in Lent

Leader   God is light; in him there is no darkness at all. If we claim to have fellowship with him yet walk in the darkness, we lie and do not live by the truth. But if we walk in the light, as he is in the light, we have fellowship with one another and the blood of Jesus, his Son, purifies us from all sin.

Silence

Leader   Lord Jesus, Light of the World, if we follow you we will never walk in darkness but have the light of life. As we come before you now, may the light of your love shine ever more brightly in our lives, banishing the gloom of sin and despair, and filling us with your grace and joy, so that others too may turn from darkness to light and acknowledge you as Lord, to the glory of your name. Amen.

SONG   *Only by grace* (Gerrit Gustafson)

Leader   Here and now, dear friends, we are God's children. We do not yet know what we will be when he appears, but we will be like him, for we will see him as he is. As we have this hope before us,

All   may we be purified, as Christ is pure.

Leader   Christ appeared to do away with sin, and in him there is no sin. As we dwell in him,

All   may we keep God's law and not do wrong.

Leader   The Son of God appeared to destroy the work of the evil one. As he is righteous,

All   may we do what is right, and not be led astray.

Leader   Those who are born of God do not continue in sin; that is the distinction between the children of God and the children of the devil. As we remain in him,

All   may we love one another as he has loved us.

READING
Luke 19:41-end

As Jesus approached Jerusalem and saw the city, he wept over it and said, 'If you, even you, had only known on this day what would bring you peace – but now it is hidden from your eyes. The days will come upon you when your enemies will build an embankment against you and encircle you and hem you in on every side. They will dash you to the ground, you and the children within your walls. They will not leave one stone on another, because you did not recognise the time of God's coming to you.'

Then he entered the Temple area and began driving out those who were selling. 'It is written,' he said to them, '"My house will be a house of prayer"; but you have made it a den of robbers.' Every day he was teaching at the Temple. But the chief priests, the teachers of the law and the leaders among the people were trying to kill him. Yet they could not find any way to do it, because all the people hung on his words.

MEDITATION

We're so familiar with the ethos of the market-place that Jesus' action in driving out the traders in the Temple courtyard may seem rather extreme. However, Jesus' point was not primarily about economic principles but spiritual ones. These stallholders weren't making an honest living, but taking advantage of the poor by selling sacrificial animals and birds at extorted prices. Although it was done in the name of religion, their real motivation was greed and power – evil wasn't only residing in God's house, but masquerading as part of it. Jesus' conflict was with the forces which were corrupting the very heart of the worship of God. If we follow the way of Jesus we too are in conflict with everything which spoils God's creation, corrupts his Church and exploits other people. Condemnation of 'the evils in society' may be necessary, but as Christians we're also called actively to confront these and work towards a better alternative. For example, the behaviour of some young people in your area may be deplorable, but could you offer or support any projects to provide a context for them to show themselves in a better light? What do you regard as evil in our world – racism, religious bigotry, dishonesty and corruption in high places, exploitation of the poor, third-world debt, environmental damage, unemployment? How do you try to challenge these? Do you support charities and aid agencies which have been set up specifically to address these issues? Are you aware of environmental issues when you do your shopping? You may feel that you can do very little, but many small contributions eventually form a much larger one. Ask God to help you recognise what you can do, however insignificant it may seem, and to give you strength and grace to act on your vision.

Leader	We kneel before Jesus, the conqueror of evil and death, at whose name every knee shall bow, to pray for our world and its needs. Victorious Lord,
All	receive our prayer.
Group A	We pray for the homeless and deprived, and for all those who seek to show them your love and care by providing shelter and the necessities of life. In your name may we work to uphold the value and worth of every human being, and ensure that no one is excluded from enjoying the life you have given them. Victorious Lord,
All	receive our prayer.
Group B	We pray for the vulnerable members of our society, the elderly or infirm, the mentally handicapped, the chronically sick, and for all who devote their energy and time to caring for them. In your name may we work to bring them your love and healing grace, and enable them to know and serve you in spite of their limitations and discomfort. Victorious Lord,
All	receive our prayer.
A	We pray for all who are dying from starvation, neglect or lack of basic medical care, particularly in third-world countries, and for all who seek to bring them relief and aid in their distress. In your name may we work to alleviate all kinds of human misery, and show your compassion to any who are in need, that they may see in us the reality of your love for them. Victorious Lord,
All	receive our prayer.
B	We pray for all young people, especially those who are victims of abuse or vulnerable to the prevailing temptations. We also commit to you all teachers, youth leaders and any whose work involves responsibility for children, their nurture and their care. In your name may we work together to make our schools and clubs places where young people can grow up in the knowledge of God and his ways, so that they in turn can fight against evil and do right. Victorious Lord,

	All	receive our prayer.
	A	We pray for all who are lonely or isolated through circumstances, or whose fears and anxieties are known to you alone. In your name may we befriend the friendless and welcome those who feel unwanted and unloved, that in you they may find a faithful friend. Victorious Lord,
	All	receive our prayer.
	B	We pray for all in government or positions of authority and influence, whose decisions direct society and affect the lives of the whole world. In your name may they follow your ways of justice and peace, acting as good stewards of our resources and demonstrating your care and love for the needy, that all may enjoy the life you have given us. Victorious Lord,
	All	receive our prayer and strengthen us to fight against evil and follow Christ for the sake of your eternal kingdom. Amen.
SONG		*Heaven shall not wait* (Iona Community)
	Leader	How great is the love the Father has shown us. In keeping a moment of silence, let us thank God for his love as we see it in Jesus Christ, and pray especially for those who need his touch on their lives.
		Silence
	Leader	We pray for our families and those we live with,
	All	Lord, give us all your love.
	Leader	For our friends and neighbours, and those whose company we enjoy,
	All	Lord, give us all your joy.
	Leader	For our colleagues and those with whom we work,
	All	Lord, give us all your strength.
	Leader	For those who cause us concern or anxiety,
	All	Lord, give us all your peace.

Leader	For those with whom we share our common faith in Jesus Christ,
All	Lord, give us all your courage to stand against evil and live for you.
Leader	We ask these things in the name of Jesus, who taught us to pray:
All	Our Father . . .
Leader	As we go into the world and face the conflict, let us bless the Lord.
All	Thanks be to God.

Third Sunday in Lent

Leader   If we endure suffering for doing right, God will bless us, for he called us to this. Christ himself suffered for us, leaving us an example so that we might follow in his steps.

Silence

Leader   Lord Jesus, suffering servant, you rule all things yet willingly gave yourself up to scorn, ill-treatment and death so that we might have eternal life. As we kneel in your presence, may we find strength to endure suffering for your sake, that walking with you in the way of the cross, we may work for your kingdom with all the energy and power of Christ within us, in whose name we pray. Amen.

SONG   *There is a Redeemer* (Melody Green)

Leader   Christ died for sins once for all, the righteous for the unrighteous, to bring us to God. Since he suffered in his body and died that we might live,

All   may we die to sin and live to righteousness.

Leader   Christ committed no sin, and no deceit was heard from his lips;

All   may we die to sin and live to righteousness.

Leader   Christ did not retaliate when insults were hurled at him;

All   may we die to sin and live to righteousness.

Leader   Christ did not make threats when he suffered, but put his trust in the one who judges rightly;

All   may we die to sin and live to righteousness.

Leader   Christ was wounded that we might be healed;

All   may we die to sin and live to righteousness.

Leader   Christ is the Shepherd and Keeper of our souls, who brought us back when we were lost;

Third Sunday in Lent

All   may we die to sin and live to righteousness, following his example and obeying his commands, so that we may rejoice when we suffer for his sake and receive the crown of glory. Amen.

READING
Luke 9:18-27

Once when Jesus was praying in private and his disciples were with him, he asked them, 'Who do the crowds say I am?' They replied, 'Some say John the Baptist, others say Elijah, and still others, that one of the prophets of long ago has come back to life'.

'But what about you?' he asked. 'Who do you say that I am?' Peter answered, 'The Christ of God'. Jesus strictly warned them not to tell this to anyone. And he said, 'The Son of Man must suffer many things and be rejected by the elders, chief priests and teachers of the law, and he must be killed and on the third day be raised to life'.

Then he said to them all: 'If anyone would come after me, he must deny himself and take up his cross daily and follow me. For whoever wants to save his life will lose it, but whoever loses his life for me will save it. What good is it for a man to gain the whole world, and yet lose or forfeit his very self? If anyone is ashamed of me and my words, the Son of Man will be ashamed of him when he comes in his glory and in the glory of the Father and of the holy angels. I tell you the truth, some who are standing here will not taste death before they see the kingdom of God.'

MEDITATION

Many of Jesus' contemporaries, including the disciples, were full of optimism that he would lead a political revolution to oust the Roman overlords from Palestine and restore the 'golden days' of the Davidic monarchy. They accepted him gladly as the Messiah, but found it hard to understand why he should have to die, destroying all their hopes for the future, so Jesus explains that what is about to happen will be the fulfilment of Scripture and the ultimate purpose of his coming to this earth. The victory of the resurrection can't be won without the suffering and conflict of the cross and death. We too can easily make the same mistake as the disciples, wanting to enjoy the blessings of the Christian life without the cost of following the way of Jesus. We baulk at the idea of 'losing our lives', or releasing our grip on something we hold dear, but don't realise that in so doing we will find something far greater and more valuable. What are you most afraid of losing – friends or popularity, wealth or lifestyle, ambition or status, personal happiness? If your life is centred on any of these rather than following Christ, then you may enjoy them in the short term but lose out ultimately by neglecting the spiritual aspect of life. What does it cost you to be a Christian? Have you ever missed out in the world's terms because of your faith, only to discover that you've gained something far greater? Ask God to help you see the things of this life in their eternal perspective, and to give you strength to face the cost of following Jesus in your own circumstances.

Leader	We turn to Jesus, the friend of sinners, who for the joy set before him endured the cross that we might receive eternal life, saying, Lord of the cross of shame,
All	help us to deny ourselves and follow you.
Leader	When we are distracted by the concerns of this world from considering your claims on our lives, give us a vision of what you suffered on our behalf. Lord of the cross of shame,
All	help us to deny ourselves and follow you.
Leader	When we are anxious or sad, fearful or wallowing in self-pity, may we feel your presence alongside us, sharing our sorrows and giving us grace to endure them. Lord of the cross of shame,
All	help us to deny ourselves and follow you.
Leader	When we are angry or upset, unable to understand your purposes and confused about where you are leading us, calm our troubled hearts and give us faith to trust you in every circumstance. Lord of the cross of shame,
All	help us to deny ourselves and follow you.
Leader	When we are tempted to give up because we can see no way out of our problems and pain, or doubt your promises for the future, fill our hearts with your hope and renew our vision of our heavenly home. Lord of the cross of shame,
All	help us to deny ourselves and follow you, that by living for you in this world we may know the joy of the world to come, for the sake of your Son, our Saviour Jesus Christ. Amen.
SONG	*Will you come and follow me* (Iona Community)

Leader	We keep silence as we remember before God all who have willingly suffered for the name of Christ, and pray that we who have seen their witness may also follow their example.
	Silence
Leader	As we return to our daily lives we bring before God the suffering and pain in his world:
Group A	We pray for all prisoners of conscience and those who have lost their freedom for doing right, that they may be given strength to stand firm in their faith and not give up the fight against wrong.
Group B	We pray for all Christians whose public affirmation of faith puts them at risk of death or persecution, that they may be given courage to remain true to you.
A	We pray for those who are anxious about a particular decision or facing a time of crisis and uncertainty, that they may be given faith to trust you to see them through their difficult circumstances.
B	We pray for those whose faith is under pressure in their family or place of work, that they may be given confidence to bear witness to your truth and love.
A	We pray for any who are suffering ill-health in body or mind, or who are burdened with the care of elderly and infirm loved ones, that they may be given healing grace and know the joy of your salvation.
B	We pray for the bereaved and lonely whose pain is known to you alone, that in their sorrow they may be given the peace of God which passes all understanding.
Leader	We commit to God our own circumstances, praying that as we walk in the way of Jesus we may accept willingly the suffering of the cross and find in it life and peace, for his name's sake. Amen.
Leader	Lord Jesus, remember us in your kingdom, as obeying your command we pray:
All	Our Father . . .
Leader	For all who have gone before us in the way of Christ and now share his eternal glory, let us bless the Lord.
All	Thanks be to God.

Fourth Sunday in Lent

Leader   All of us reflect the glory of the Lord, which, coming from the Lord who is the Spirit, transforms us into his likeness in an ever greater degree of glory.

Silence

Leader   Lord Jesus, God's own beloved Son, before your death you appeared in the radiance of the Father to your disciples that they might see your majesty. As we bow the knee before you, may we too recognise your glory and be changed more and more into your likeness, so that our faith is strengthened and our confidence increased, for your name's sake. Amen.

SONG   *Laudate Dominum* (Taizé Community)

Leader   We stand before God because we have confidence in him through Christ. We are not able to claim anything for ourselves for he alone makes us able to serve the New Covenant. The written law brings death,

All   but the Spirit gives life.

Leader   The written law was carved on stone tablets, and God's glory appeared when it was given, even though it was fading from Moses' face,

All   but the activity of the Spirit brings a greater glory which lasts for ever.

Leader   The written law is not unveiled to those with closed minds for they have not been joined to Christ,

All   but, where the Spirit of the Lord is present, there is freedom.

Leader   All of us reflect God's glory, that same glory which comes from the Lord, who is the Spirit,

All   and the Spirit transforms us more and more into his likeness, with ever-increasing glory.

Fourth Sunday in Lent

READING
Luke 9:28-36

Jesus took Peter, James and John with him and went up to a mountain to pray. As he was praying, the appearance of his face changed, and his clothes became as bright as a flash of lightning. Two men, Moses and Elijah, appeared in glorious splendour, talking with Jesus. They spoke about his departure, which he was about to bring to fulfilment at Jerusalem. Peter and his companions were very sleepy, but when they became fully awake, they saw his glory and the two men standing with him. As the men were leaving Jesus, Peter said to him, 'Master, it is good for us to be here. Let us put up three shelters – one for you, one for Moses and one for Elijah.' (He did not know what he was saying.)

While he was speaking, a cloud appeared and enveloped them, and they were afraid as they entered the cloud. A voice came from the cloud, saying, 'This is my Son, whom I have chosen; listen to him'. When the voice had spoken, they found that Jesus was alone. The disciples kept this to themselves and told no one at the time what they had seen.

MEDITATION

Experiences of God's glory don't come to order. The disciples had gone with Jesus into the hills to pray, so the sight of him radiant in glory, speaking with Moses and Elijah about his coming death in Jerusalem, must have been not only breathtaking but also very disturbing. This experience seems not to have lasted for long, and once it was over they had to return to the other disciples and the realities of life. The transfiguration of Jesus wasn't an antidote to his suffering and death, but served instead to put them in the context of the Father's purposes. We might be tempted to dismiss such a revelation as the product of an overactive imagination, or, having received one, to spend our time trying to recapture it. But God gives such experiences to set our ministry in his name in its eternal context, and to provide a stimulus for our witness and service. Often he does so 'out of the blue', particularly when we've set aside time to be alone with him in prayer. Have you ever experienced Jesus revealed in majesty and glory, and how have you reacted to him? Do you feel tempted to seek out such experiences or reject them as purely subjective? Have these occasions given you impetus to live the Christian life more boldly, and faith to follow the way of Christ, even when this might involve suffering or hardship? Ask God to show you how you can reflect his glory more clearly to the world around, both in your words and actions.

Leader	We bow before the glorious presence of Jesus, the true light who came to this world to give light to everyone, saying, 'the glory of the Lord has been revealed',
All	may all people see it together.
Group A	Where there is hatred and bitterness between individuals, families, communities and nations, may God's glory be revealed.
Group B	Where there is violence and warfare causing injury, death and destruction, may God's glory be revealed.
A	Where there is hopelessness and despair with no sense of direction or hope for the future, may God's glory be revealed.
B	Where there is apathy and self-centredness with no care for the interests or hurts of others, may God's glory be revealed.
A	Where there is oppression and injustice, using the poor and vulnerable to increase power and wealth, may God's glory be revealed.
B	Where there is exploitation and greed, degrading human beings and spoiling creation, may God's glory be revealed.
A	Where there is loneliness and fear, creating isolation and blocking out peace, may God's glory be revealed.
B	Where there is illness of body or mind, depression or grief, may God's glory be revealed.
Leader	The light of Christ has come into this world. Whoever lives by the truth comes into the light so that it will be clear that his actions are of God. In our lives at home or in the world, at work or at leisure, the glory of the Lord will be revealed,
All	and all people will see it together.

SONG *Meekness and majesty* (Graham Kendrick)

Leader   In a time of silence we lift our hearts in prayer that the light of Christ will shine into the dark places of our own lives and of the world around, that his glory will be seen by all people.

Silence

Leader	We ask God to reveal his glory to us in his Son Jesus Christ, and through us to all those we meet in our daily lives. When we encounter lives twisted by hatred and hostility, Lord,
All	let your love shine through us.
Leader	When we see pain and suffering, Lord,
All	let your healing flow through us.
Leader	When we confront doubt and despair, Lord,
All	let your hope be seen in us.
Leader	When we face sadness and grief, Lord,
All	let your joy rise up in us.
Leader	When we contend with fear and anxiety, Lord,
All	let your peace bring calm through us.
Leader	As we offer in your name consolation, understanding and love to those around us, may we be transformed by your Spirit to become more like you, our Saviour and friend, and so be strengthened in faith and hope, through Jesus Christ our Lord, who taught his followers to pray:
All	Our Father . . .
Leader	In our lives each day
All	may you be glorified.
Leader	In our lives together
All	may you be glorified.
Leader	In our lives throughout this earthly pilgrimage
All	may you be glorified, until we worship you for ever around your throne. Amen.
Leader	Let us bless the Lord.
All	Thanks be to God.

Passion Sunday

Leader   Jesus said: 'Anyone who loves his life loses it, while anyone who hates his life in this world will keep it for eternal life. Whoever serves me must follow me, and where I am, my servant will also be.'

Silence

Leader   Lord Jesus, Redeemer of the world, you left your home in glory to be lifted up from the earth so that all people might be drawn to you. As we look on you suffering humiliation and dying in agony on the cross, may we also see you there in power and majesty, that in recognising you as conqueror of evil and death we may know our sins forgiven and enter into eternal life with you. Amen.

SONG   *Come and see* (Graham Kendrick)

Leader   Just as you have received Christ Jesus as Lord, continue to live in him; do not let your minds be captured by deceptive philosophy, which depends on human tradition and the principles of this world rather than on Christ.

Group A   In Christ the complete being of the Godhead lives in bodily form;

Group B   we have been brought to completion in him.

A   In Christ we have been purified by the removal of our sinful nature;

B   we have been buried with him in baptism and raised with him through faith in the power of God.

A   In Christ God has made us alive by forgiving all our sins;

B   he took away the written law which condemns us, nailing it to the cross.

A   In Christ the powers and authorities of this world are disarmed;

B   he made a public spectacle of them, leading them as captives in his victory procession.

Leader	Since we have died with Christ to this world, let us therefore no longer behave as though we belonged to it, but set our hearts on things above.
READING Mark 10:32-45	They were on their way up to Jerusalem, with Jesus leading the way, and the disciples were astonished, while those who followed were afraid. Again he took the twelve aside and told them what was going to happen to him. 'We are going up to Jerusalem,' he said, 'and the Son of Man will be betrayed to the chief priests and teachers of the law. They will condemn him to death and will turn him over to the Gentiles, who will mock him and spit on him, flog him and kill him. Three days later he will rise.' Then James and John, the sons of Zebedee, came to him. 'Teacher,' they said, 'we want you to do for us whatever we ask.' 'What do you want me to do for you?' he asked. They replied, 'Let one of us sit at your right and the other at your left in your glory'. 'You don't know what you are asking', Jesus said. 'Can you drink the cup I drink, or be baptised with the baptism I am baptised with?' 'We can', they answered. Jesus said to them, 'You will drink the cup I drink, and be baptised with the baptism I am baptised with, but to sit at my right or left is not for me to grant. These places belong to those for whom they have been prepared.' When the ten heard about this they became indignant with James and John. Jesus called them together and said, 'You know that those who are regarded as rulers of the Gentiles lord it over them, and their high officials exercise authority over them. Not so with you. Instead, whoever wants to become great among you must be your servant, and whoever wants to be first must be slave of all. For even the Son of Man did not come to be served but to serve, and to give his life as a ransom for many.'
MEDITATION	All four Gospels portray the disciples as decidedly human and fallible. James and John were two of the closest to Jesus, and not long before this incident they had witnessed his transfiguration. Yet none of this prevents them squabbling with the other disciples about their future status in the kingdom of God. Perhaps they thought their closer relationship to Jesus entitled them to greater status, or possibly they felt their efforts deserved more recognition. Whatever the cause, the effect was to annoy the other ten

disciples and leave Jesus with a dispute to resolve. Despite all they'd seen and learned over the previous three years, they hadn't yet understood that to share Jesus' status also meant sharing his suffering, nor that in God's kingdom the values of this world are completely reversed. Those who follow Jesus aren't exempt from the temptation to status-seeking, and the divisions it causes have torn the Church apart throughout its history. Too often we ask what we can do to project our image better or increase our resources, instead of asking what God wants us to do to serve those around us. The only antidote is for us to turn the world's standards and attitudes upside down, as Jesus did, and follow the way of willing service to others which leads to true greatness. How willing are you to accept suffering or inconvenience for the sake of God's kingdom, and what would you find hardest to sacrifice? How do you exercise authority over others, and acknowledge those in authority over you? How willing are you to accept the role of servant for the sake of God's kingdom, and what might this involve? Ask God to help you overcome the temptation to lord it over others, or influence them to your own advantage, so that you can serve them without any ulterior motives.

Leader	We approach the throne of the Servant King, who kneels and washes his disciples' feet, saying, Lord Jesus, wash us clean,
All	and make us alive in you.
Leader	When we feel tempted to turn away from suffering and choose the easy path, Lord Jesus, wash us clean,
All	and make us alive in you.
Leader	When we feel tempted to seek personal recognition and standing above other people, Lord Jesus, wash us clean,
All	and make us alive with you.
Leader	When we feel tempted to further our own interests and disregard the needs of those around us, Lord Jesus, wash us clean,
All	and make us alive in you.
Leader	When we feel tempted to pursue power and put aside our calling to serve others in your name, Lord Jesus, wash us clean,

All	and make us alive in you.	
Leader	As you have washed our feet and set us an example to follow,	
All	may we do for others what you have done for us, for the sake of your kingdom. Amen.	

SONG *From heaven you came* (Graham Kendrick)

Leader We bring to God in the quiet of our hearts our prayers for all those who with us are committed to serving him faithfully without counting the cost.

Silence

Leader We ask God to put within us the mind of Christ, and make us willing to serve him wherever he gives us the opportunity. In our homes and families

All may we serve you joyfully.

Leader At work and at leisure

All may we serve you faithfully.

Leader In times of stress and exertion

All may we serve you loyally.

Leader In times of quietness and reflection

All may we serve you devotedly.

Leader In times of sorrow and times of joy

All may we serve you wholeheartedly, seeking no reward other than knowing we are doing your will. Amen.

Leader Following the way of Jesus, we pray as he taught us:

All Our Father . . .

Leader For Jesus, who stoops in humility to wash our feet,

All let us bless the Lord.

Leader For Jesus, the Servant King, who gave his life as a ransom for many,

All let us bless the Lord. Thanks be to God.

Palm Sunday

Leader Your attitude to one another should arise out of your life in Christ Jesus, who, though he was in his very nature divine, did not grasp at equality with God but made himself nothing, taking the form of a servant.

Silence

Leader Lord Jesus, Son of David and Son of God, you humbled yourself by taking our humanity and obediently accepting death on a cross. Now you are exalted to the highest place and have the name which is above all other names, to which every knee must bow. As we offer ourselves to you in worship, may we also follow your example of humility and obedience so that in dying to sin, we may rise with you to eternal life, Amen.

SONG *You are the king of glory* (Mavis Ford)

Leader We do not preach the Gospel with words of human wisdom, lest the cross of Christ be emptied of its power. The message of the cross is folly to those who are perishing,

All but to us who are being saved it is the power of God.

Leader God has made foolish the cleverness of the wise man, the scholar and the philosopher,

All for the world cannot know God through wisdom.

Leader Through the folly of what is preached

All God is pleased to save those who believe.

Leader The Jews demand signs, while the Greeks seek after wisdom,

All but we preach Christ crucified.

Leader The cross is a stumbling-block to the Jews and folly to the Gentiles,

All but to those who are called, whether Jew or Gentile, it is the power and wisdom of God.

Leader	The foolishness of God is infinitely wiser than human wisdom,
All	his weakness is infinitely greater than human strength.

READING
Matthew 21:1-13

As they approached Jerusalem and came to Bethphage on the Mount of Olives, Jesus sent two disciples, saying to them, 'Go to the village ahead of you, and at once you will find a donkey tied there, with her colt by her. Untie them, and bring them to me. If anyone says anything to you, tell him that the Lord needs them, and he will send them right away.' This took place to fulfil what was spoken through the prophet: 'Say to the daughter of Zion, "See your King comes to you, gentle and riding on a donkey, on a colt, the foal of a donkey".'

The disciples went and did as Jesus had instructed them. They brought the donkey and the colt, placed their cloaks on them, and Jesus sat on them. A very large crowd spread their cloaks on the road, while others cut branches from the trees and spread them on the road. The crowds that went ahead of him, and those that followed shouted, 'Hosanna to the Son of David! Blessed is he who comes in the name of the Lord! Hosanna in the highest!' When Jesus entered, the whole city was stirred and asked, 'Who is this?' The crowds answered, 'This is Jesus, the prophet from Nazareth in Galilee'.

Jesus entered the temple area and drove out all who were buying and selling there. He overturned the tables of the money changers and the benches of those selling doves. 'It is written,' he said to them, '"My house will be called a house of prayer", but you are making it a den of robbers.'

MEDITATION

Although Jesus knew he was entering Jerusalem to face certain death, nothing could have seemed less likely than his crucifixion only a few days later. Many people would have identified his entry into the city on a donkey with Zechariah's prophecy, and so they acclaimed him as their king, the one who would restore the Davidic monarchy and challenge the authority of the Romans. The cheering and celebration of the crowds are in marked contrast to the jeering and humiliation which greeted him so soon afterwards. It would have been easy for Jesus to bask in the popular acclaim, but he knew how quickly this could change, and didn't allow it to deflect him from his mission. Immediately he went to the Temple, and banished the traders in the courtyard, issuing a direct challenge to the corruption and rottenness which were debasing the whole system of religion. Popularity can seem very attractive in the short term, but it doesn't last long and usually gets in the way of achieving anything worthwhile. Jesus kept his mission in full view, never moving away from it or allowing himself to be distracted. How important is popularity to you, and what lengths will you go to in order to achieve it? On what issues would you risk unpopularity with your family, friends or colleagues? Where can you challenge the prevailing corruption and evil, and how might you go about it? Ask God for courage to resist the attractions of short-term acclaim and to oppose everything which is contrary to his kingdom.

Leader We stand in the presence of Jesus our Saviour, who for our sake willingly followed the path of suffering and pain to the cross, and we ask for strength to share that way with him.

Group A For the times when we are tempted to take the broad path of popularity and acclaim which leads to destruction, Lord give us your will.

Group B For the times when we are tempted to turn aside from the narrow road of service and obedience, Lord give us your resolve.

A For the times when we find ourselves in conflict with evil and corruption, Lord give us your anger.

B For the times when we are called to uphold your standards of righteousness and justice, Lord give us your zeal.

A For the times when we are confronted with fear and despair, Lord give us your hope.

B For the times when we see misery and pain all around us, Lord give us your compassion.

A For the times when the road ahead of us seems rough and impassable, Lord give us your courage.

B For the times when we hear you calling us onwards in our pilgrimage, Lord give us your vision.

Leader	Help us so to walk with you in the way of the cross, that in this world we may find joy and peace in faithful service, and in the world to come eternal life, for your holy name's sake. Amen.	

SONG *I, the Lord of sea and sky (Here I am, Lord)* (Dan Schutte)

Leader In quietness and trust we find our strength. As we wait on the Lord we commit to him the way ahead of us, praying for guidance to know where we should be going, and confidence that he will lead us in the right paths.

Silence

Leader We pray for all Christian leaders both within the church and in other fields, that they will fulfil their duty to defend the truth and lead us in the pilgrim way. Lord, by your mercy,

All keep them faithful.

Leader We pray for all governments and authorities, that under your guidance they will fulfil their responsibilities fairly and rule us justly. Lord, by your mercy,

All keep them righteous.

Leader We pray for all aid-workers and carers, that they will tend those to whom they minister with compassion and devotion. Lord, by your mercy,

All keep them kind-hearted.

Leader We pray for all teachers and those who work with young people, that they will nurture them in your ways and guide them with your love. Lord, by your mercy,

All keep them strong.

Leader We pray for all whose pilgrimage is hard and unrewarding, that they will not lose faith in you but trust you to see them through. Lord, by your mercy,

All keep them hopeful.

Leader Keep us steadfast in faith and firm in hope as we run the race before us with our eyes fixed on Jesus, who taught us to pray:

Palm Sunday

All   Our Father . . .

Leader   For strength for today and bright hope for tomorrow, let us bless the Lord.

All   Thanks be to God.

FOLENS HISTORY

THE MAKING OF THE UK

RICHARD ALLISON
CAROLE BROWN

Acknowledgements

The authors and publishers would like to thank the following for permission to reproduce photographs and other material:

By permission of The British Library (8E)
Courtesy of the Trustees of the British Museum (16B; 18B)
City of Bristol Record Office (Reference 17562/1) (20B)
Crown Copyright (3B)
Jarrold Publishing (1D; 22B)
Mansell Collection (11A; 14C; 14D; 20H; 21C)
By permission of The Marquess of Cholmondeley (22B)
The National Portrait Gallery (2A; 2E; 3A; 4A; 4B; 5A; 6A; 6B; 6C; 7A; 7C; 7D; 8C; 9B; 11B; 11E; 13A; 15A; 16A; 18A; 19A; 19B; 22A; 23A; 24E)
Public Record Office (11E; 11F)
The Shakespeare Birthplace Trust (1D)

Illustrators:

Denby Designs
Jillian Luff of Bitmap Graphics
Paul Nicholls

Cover:

Design - Tanglewood Graphics, Broadway House, The Broadway, London SW19
Illustration - Abacus Publicity Limited

The publishers have made every effort to contact copyright holders but this has not always been possible. If any have been overlooked we will be pleased to make any necessary arrangements.

Folens books are protected by international copyright laws. All rights reserved. The copyright of all materials in this book, except where otherwise stated, remains the property of the publisher and author(s). No part of this publication may be reproduced, stored in a retrieval system, or transmitted, in any form or by any means, for whatever purpose, without the written permission of Folens Limited.

© 1990 Folens Limited, on behalf of the author.

First published 1990 by Folens Limited, Dunstable and Dublin.
Folens Limited, Albert House, Apex Business Centre, Boscombe Road, Dunstable LU5 4RL, England.

ISBN 1 85276 122 9

Printed in Singapore by Craft Print.

CONTENTS

Unit	Title	Page
1	MERRIE ENGLAND	4
2	HENRY VIII	7
3	CARDINAL WOLSEY	10
4	THE REFORMATION	12
5	THE GREAT DISSOLUTION	14
6	EDWARD VI AND MARY TUDOR	16
7	THE YOUNG QUEEN ELIZABETH	18
8	ELIZABETH AND MARY	20
9	THE SPANISH ARMADA OF 1588	22
10	THE RISE OF THE GENTRY	25
11	THE GUNPOWDER PLOT	28
12	THE LIFE OF THE POOR	31
13	CHARLES I	33
14	THE ENGLISH CIVIL WAR	35
15	OLIVER CROMWELL	37
16	THE MERRY MONARCH	39
17	THE PLAGUE & FIRE OF LONDON	41
18	THE GLORIOUS REVOLUTION	44
19	WILLIAM AND MARY	46
20	THE SLAVE TRADE	49
21	GEORGIAN LONDON	52
22	SIR ROBERT WALPOLE	54
23	BONNIE PRINCE CHARLIE	56
24	SCIENCE AND SUPERSTITION	58
25	THE FORMATION OF THE UK	61
	Index	62
	Timeline	64

1. MERRIE ENGLAND

1000
1100
1200
1300
1400
1500
1600
1700
1800
1900
2000

Targets

* To investigate the reasons for the popularity of this period.
* To consider our images of the past in general.

The Tudor period is one of the most attractive periods to anyone who likes exploring English history through books, plays or visits to places of interest.

But why does it have such a popular appeal? By looking at these pages carefully, you should be able to find out.

The People

Henry VIII and Elizabeth I are among the best known English monarchs. Their portraits show strong and powerful leaders who are easily recognisable 400 years later.

Other figures like Mary Queen of Scots, Francis Drake, Walter Raleigh and Anne Boleyn are also very famous, possibly because of incidents which have been told to every generation of children since. Such historical characters may also have been used as the basis for nursery rhymes: Little Boy Blue may have represented Cardinal Wolsey while Jack Horner was said to have helped Henry VIII to find the deeds of the great abbey of Glastonbury. As a reward he received a 'plum manor' from the dissolution.

A modern day pub sign - 'The King's Head'.

? What is the connection between this sign and the Tudor period?

Shakespeare's birthplace, Stratford-upon-Avon.

Viewpoints

The Events

Like the 20th century, the Tudor period saw rapid changes. Henry VIII founded the Church of England. Elizabeth's seamen defeated the Armada and made expeditions to America, Russia and India. Trade and settlement developed as a result. Parliament emerged as a powerful part of the government. The population doubled and industry grew, especially textiles, iron and coal. A new era seemed to be dawning as medieval castles became redundant, the monasteries disappeared and Europeans sailed around the world. Changes bring excitement and conflict - important ingredients for any good story.

Elizabethan England was a land made up of small villages. These communities seemed to have lived in harmony with nature, enjoying the simple pleasures of drinking, feasting and dancing on the green. An urban environment far from fields and fresh air was only found in London. Despite the facts about inflation, enclosure of common land and the rising number of beggars and criminals, the image of Merrie England as a green and pleasant land remains very powerful.

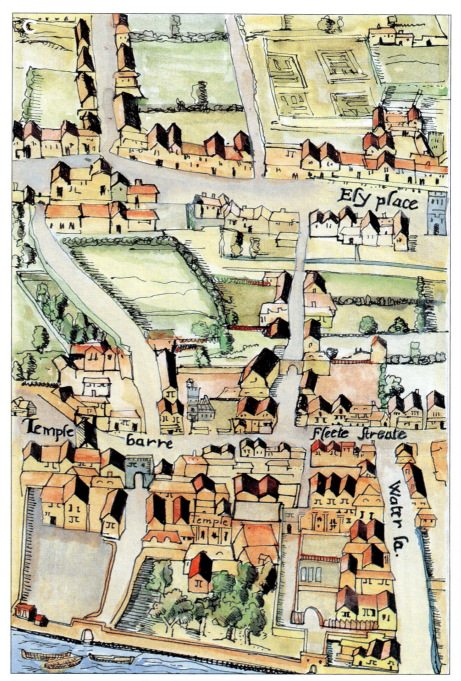

A map showing part of London in Tudor times.

Can you find any names to help you to locate this area?

The Lifestyle

Tudor houses, with their black and white timber frames, small casement windows and solid wooden furniture are close to the modern ideal of a home in the country. The style has influenced many houses and cricket pavilions in the 20th century.

Viewpoints

D

The Bard of Avon.

William Shakespeare

The English language reached a peak in the late 16th century. The poems and plays of Shakespeare and his contemporaries remain the most effective and eloquent expressions of feelings and beliefs about all aspects of human experience. In London's new theatres actors brought these ideas to life for a wide section of society. Printing preserved their lines so that these dramas could be performed at court or the most remote country town, and in every age since then. Of course it is interesting to note that Shakespeare used English history as the basis for many of his plays. His version of these events gives us a good understanding of how the Tudor government viewed the past: villainous Yorkists like Richard III and brave Lancastrians like Henry V. When he gave Elizabeth's ancestor, John of Gaunt, the lines about the country which his audience loved most (**E**), Shakespeare was helping to build up an image of England which still inspires many people today.

CORE ACTIVITIES

1 Look again at the People section.
  ● What incidents do you associate with each of the characters listed there?

2 **C** is a map of London in Tudor times.
  ● How does it differ from a modern one?
  ● What details can you find which give an idea of what this area was like in Tudor times?

3 Look again at the four sections in this unit. Each is a possible reason why the Tudor period is popular.
  ● In a small group, discuss each reason.
  ● Try to decide:
    - which reason is probably the most important
    - which reason is the least important
  ● Can you suggest a fifth reason for the popularity of the Tudor period?

E

'This royal throne of kings, this sceptered isle,
This earth of majesty, this seat of Mars,
This other Eden, demi-paradise,
This fortress built by Nature for herself
Against infection and the hand of war.
This happy breed of men, this little world,
This precious stone set in the silver sea....
This blessed plot, this earth, this realm, this England.'

Richard II (Act II, Scene i). Shakespeare.

 What view of England is presented here?

F

'Each change of many colour'd life he drew,
Exhausted worlds, and then imagin'd new'.

A comment on Shakespeare made by Dr. Samuel Johnson (1709-84).

 Try to explain this view of Shakespeare to a friend.

EXTENSION ACTIVITIES

1 This period is often thought of as very popular.
  ● Do you agree with this suggestion? Give reasons for your anwser.
  ● What other historical times do you find interesting and why?

2 Read Dr. Johnson's comment, **F**.
  ● In what ways could it be applied to the period as well as Shakespeare?

2. HENRY VIII

Targets

* To investigate sources dealing with his character and appearance.
* To consider the reliability of this evidence and the views of some historians.

Henry VIII is one of the most famous figures in English history. His claims to fame include marrying six wives, making himself head of the Church in England and enriching himself from the destruction of the monasteries. He is also remembered because of his public image which is preserved for us in the pictures painted by artists like Holbein.

Henry became king when he was 17. His father, Henry VII, left him plenty of money and a peaceful kingdom. It was the first time for over a century that a monarch came to the throne without facing the threat of attack by a powerful rival. It seemed to be a time of hope and promise for the future.

Henry VIII as a young king.

? *What impression of the young king is given by this painting?*

B

Could you but see how nobly he is bearing himself, how wise he is, his love for all that is good and right, and specially his love of learning, you would need no wings to fly into the light of this new risen...star....how proud our people are of their new sovereign...Heaven smiles, earth triumphs, and flows with milk and honey and nectar. This king of ours is no seeker after gold, or gems, or mines of silver. He desires only the fame of virtue and eternal life.

Letter from Lord Mountjoy, a courtier, 1509.

? *Explain this view of Henry VIII to a friend.*

When his elder brother, Arthur, died in 1502, Henry's father decided to keep him at court under strict supervision. He learnt to ride, hunt and joust, but was given no official duties to perform himself. Henry married his brother's widow, Catherine of Aragon, who was five years his senior.

Evidence

C

His Majesty is the handsomest potentate (ruler) I ever set eyes on; above the usual height, with an extremely fine calf to his leg, his complexion very fair and bright, with auburn hair combed straight and short, in the French fashion, and a round face so very beautiful, that it would become a pretty woman... He speaks French, English, and Latin, and a little Italian, plays well on the lute and harpsichord, sings from book at sight, draws the bow with greater strength than any man in England, and jousts marvellously. Believe me, he is in every respect a most accomplished Prince.

Dispatch from the Venetian ambassador, 1515.

D

If all the pictures and patterns of a merciless Prince were lost in the World, they might all again be painted to the life, out of the story of this King.

The Historie of the World. Sir Walter Raleigh, c.1610.

 Was this written before or after Henry's death?

In Tudor times the death penalty was frequently imposed by judges, especially for convicted traitors and heretics. Therefore it may not seem surprising that Henry had two of his wives, his leading advisers, Thomas More and Thomas Cromwell, and some survivors of the Royal House of York beheaded.

Henry believed that winning glory in battle was a vital part of being a successful king. He squandered most of his inheritance on wars with France early in his reign.

To ensure their loyalty Henry gave his leading nobles posts in the royal household. Tournaments, hunting and great feasts made court life enjoyable. The king moved between his palaces at Westminster, Greenwich, Richmond and Windsor and only moved far from his capital for hunting in late summer. There was always plenty of gossip about the king's favourites and mistresses. Not surprisingly in this round of pleasure Henry relied on a few important advisers to carry out the routine duties of his government; he even asked others to read books for him and give him a summary so he could learn about new ideas with the minimum of time and effort.

Henry VIII near the end of his reign.

 *How does this view of Henry differ from that shown in **A**?*

Evidence

As he grew older he became fat. In 1536 his horse fell on top of him during a tournament and he lay unconscious for two hours. An ulcer developed on his thigh which became swollen and gave him terrible pain in his later years.

He decided to build a completely new palace called Nonsuch in Surrey from some of the wealth taken from the Church. A whole village was destroyed to make way for this elaborate building with turrets, pinnacles and ornate chimney pots. The statues included Henry on his throne, trampling a lion, surrounded by Roman emperors. The details included a 'close stool (toilet) for the use of the King's Majesty', costing over £6. It had a wooden seat, back and elbows, padded with down, covered in black velvet with a fringe of silk. The accounts also mention a bowl and cistern, showing that this was a proper flushing water closet, perhaps the first in English history.

G

For all his power to dazzle, for all the charm and bonhomie (good humour) which he could undoubtedly sometimes show, and for all the affection which he could certainly give and receive, it is difficult to think of any truly generous or selfless action performed by him.

Henry VIII. J.J. Scarisbrick, 1968.

H

He is a wonderful man and has wonderful people around him but he is an old fox.

The French Ambassador, 1538.

 What do you think the French Ambassador means?

F

The plain truth is that he was a most intolerable ruffian, a disgrace to human nature, and a blot of blood and grease upon the History of England.

A Child's History of England. Charles Dickens, 1854.

EXTENSION ACTIVITY

1 Look at sources A to H again.
- Working in a small group, discuss each of them in turn. Think about:
  - what each tells us about Henry
  - how reliable they might be
  - what further types of evidence and points of view would help you to reach a firm conclusion about Henry's character and personality

CORE ACTIVITY

1 Look carefully at all the evidence in this unit.
- Describe in your own words:
  - Henry's physical appearance
  - his character and personality
  - his view of how a king should appear and behave

3. CARDINAL WOLSEY

Target

* To examine the character and motives of Wolsey and Henry VIII.
* To consider why Wolsey fell from power in 1529.

We have seen how Henry VIII tended to rely on others to manage his government. The king's first chief minister was also the leading figure in the English Church. Thomas Wolsey was a butcher's son from Ipswich who became chaplain to Henry VII.

The new king decided to press an ancient claim to the French throne and Wolsey organised the expedition in 1513 which brought the capture of Tournai. Soon he had Henry's trust as his chief adviser, negotiating treaties and making foreign policy. Wolsey's rewards were the main posts in the Church as they became vacant: Archbishop of York, Bishop of Tournai, Lincoln, Bath and Wells and Durham, as well as Cardinal and the Pope's ambassador to England. His wealth began to rival that of the king himself when in 1521 he also became abbot of the richest monastery, St. Alban's.

The Great Cardinal
The enormous wealth and power of Wolsey was bound to bring jealousy. 'This Cardinal is the person who rules both the King and the entire kingdom' wrote the Venetian ambassador in 1519. His new palace at Hampton Court, his extravagant lifestyle and almost total control of royal finances, justice and the Church provided an example of the worldliness and corruption of the clergy to many people. However, as long as he had the confidence and trust of Henry, Wolsey was safe.

Cardinal Wolsey.

Hampton Court Palace.

C

His foreign policy, often brilliant ... resulted in the isolation of England, the enmity of both Spain and France, and the king's failure to get his divorce.

England under the Tudors.
G.R. Elton, 1955.

Causation and Motivation

Wolsey the Diplomat

Wolsey tried to make alliances with Spain and the Holy Roman Empire against France. In 1518 he successfully persuaded all the leading powers of western Europe to sign a general peace treaty in London in which they promised to unite against the invasion of the Turks in Central Europe.

For a short time Wolsey could claim to be the leading international peacemaker but soon war broke out between France and the Empire, which now included Spain. Wolsey knew that England could not afford costly expeditions against the French so he arranged a meeting between Henry VIII and the king of France in 1520. This lavish event near Calais became known as 'The Field of the Cloth of Gold'. Over 5 000 people and hundreds of tents and pavilions were transported across the channel. Amid splendid pageantry, the two kings jousted and feasted and Wolsey preached a sermon on peace. However, no treaty resulted and Wolsey could not prevent England being dragged into an expensive alliance with the Emperor Charles V against France.

The King's Divorce

In 1525 Henry began an affair with Anne Boleyn. He was also convinced that he needed a son to succeed him. Queen Catherine was now 40 and her only surviving child was the ten year old Princess Mary. A divorce required the agreement of the Pope. However, Rome was dominated by Catherine's uncle, Emperor Charles. The arguments dragged on for years and in 1529 a Papal court was set up in London with Wolsey and an Italian cardinal presiding. Catherine urged that the case should be tried in Rome and the Pope agreed. Wolsey's influence had proved inadequate and his enemies saw their chance to remove him.

Wolsey had already handed over Hampton Court to try to keep Henry's favour. Now it was too late; for the first time he visited his archbishopric of York but was soon ordered to return south to face a charge of treason. He died on the journey in November 1530.

D

Wolsey paid the penalty not, as he claimed upon his deathbed, of having served his king better than his God, but of having served himself better than his king.

Tudor England. S. Bindoff, 1950.

 What do you think this comment means?

E

Wolsey ... became so proud that he considered himself the peer of kings. He soon began to use a golden chair, a golden cushion, a golden cloth on his table, and, when he was walking, to have the hat, symbol of the rank of Cardinal, carried before him by a servant, raised up like some holy idol or other ... Thus Wolsey, with his arrogance and ambition, raised against himself the hatred of the whole people and, in his hostility towards nobles and common folk, procured their great irritation at his vainglory. His own odiousness (hatefulness) was truly complete, because he claimed he could undertake himself almost all public duties.

Polydore Vergil, a court historian of Henry VIII.

CORE ACTIVITY

1 Think about Wolsey.
- How did he become so powerful?
- What was he trying to do in his foreign policy?
- Why was he unpopular with:
  - other churchmen?
  - courtiers?
- What were the reasons for his fall from power?

EXTENSION ACTIVITY

1 Look through this unit.
- Make a list of the mistakes Wolsey made during the whole period.
- Which of these were the main reasons for his fall from power?
- Discuss these in a small group and see how far you can agree upon a final list of reasons.

4. THE REFORMATION

Targets

* To investigate the causes of the Reformation in England.

The search for truth in history is like a game of 'pass the parcel'. Each new piece of reliable evidence allows us to remove one more wrapper to get closer to understanding what really happened. Of course in the party game we can see when the prize is won. In history we are never totally certain.

How and why did Henry VIII change the history of Christianity in England? Some of the reasons have to do with Henry himself; others are connected with changes going on in the Church and society generally.

In 1529 Henry VIII wanted to marry Anne Boleyn and have a legitimate male heir but the Pope would not grant him a divorce from Queen Catherine. Henry therefore decided to become head of the Church in England and give himself permission to marry again.

Catherine of Aragon.

 What sort of impression of Catherine does the artist seem to be giving?

Printing spread new ideas and gave many more people the chance to read the Bible in their own language instead of Latin. Priests became less important as the link between God and the ordinary believer. Soon the faults of the Catholic Church such as selling Indulgences to forgive sins were more widely criticised. The power of the Pope himself was challenged by priests like Martin Luther in Germany. They wanted to share in running the Church, like the first Christians. These reformers or 'protestants' gained support among all ranks of society.

Thomas Cranmer, Archbishop of Canterbury, Anne's father, the Earl of Wiltshire, and the king's new chief adviser, Thomas Cromwell, were all 'reformers'. The king himself never changed his own beliefs. He had written a book attacking Luther. As a result the Pope gave him the title 'Defender of the Faith'.

Causation

When you start an arguement do you know what the final result will be? Most people are not cold and calculating when they begin a dispute. They tend to follow their emotions as much as their reasoning and common sense.

Henry's feelings in 1529 are fairly clear, at least as far as Anne was concerned. We can trace three main stages in the royal takeover of the English Church.

Anne Boleyn.

 What evidence does this official portrait give us about Anne's appearance?

Stage 1: 1527 - 1529
Henry tried negotiating with the Pope.

Stage 2: 1529 - 1532
From November 1529 he began to use threats. Parliament was allowed to list its complaints against:

- priests who held several livings (posts) and ignored their duties;
- clergy who charged high fees for wills and Church services;
- the large amount of Church land which was not farmed properly;
- the heavy fines imposed in Church courts.

Henry claimed that it was his royal duty to correct such faults. He fined the Church for its misdeeds and made the clergy acknowledge his authority over them. The Pope was unmoved.

Stage 3: 1532 - 1533
From 1532, with the help of Cromwell, Henry drew up the laws which Parliament passed to make him 'Supreme Head of the Church of England'. 55 opponents, including Bishop John Fisher and the chancellor, Thomas More, were executed.

In 1533 Henry married Anne who gave birth to a daughter, Elizabeth. Less than three years later the new queen was found guilty of adultery and treason. She was beheaded by the sword.

CORE ACTIVITY

1 The events described in this unit mark the start of the Reformation in England.
   - What part was played by:
     - Thomas Cromwell?
     - Anne Boleyn?
     - Parliament?
     (CLUE TO SUCCESS: Some people have an indirect rather than active part to play)

EXTENSION ACTIVITY

1 Some historians argue that even if the Pope had granted Henry a divorce, the circumstances would have forced the king to take control of the English Church.
   - What evidence can you find in this and the previous unit to support this view?

5. THE GREAT DISSOLUTION

1000
1100
1200
1300
1400
1500
1600
1700
1800
1900
2000

Targets

* To consider the reasons for the dissolution.
* To evaluate some primary evidence on the situation in the monasteries.

Having made himself head of the Church, with Cromwell as his deputy or vicar-general, Henry VIII was free to reform the Church. The 825 monasteries, nunneries and friaries were all directly obedient to the Pope. So Henry's motive was to destroy them and acquire their treasure and property.

One way was to show that the monks and nuns were not behaving like good Christians. Cromwell sent out his commissioners to question them and list their property. This information produced a book called the Valor Ecclesiasticus (Valuation of the Church). Two Acts of Parliament gave the king the legal right to dissolve these religious houses. The process was completed by 1540.

Although five abbots were executed the operation was fairly peaceful and most monks and nuns were given pensions. Much of the land was sold to the king's supporters who thus gained a vested interest in the Reformation.

B

Ye shall receive a bag of relics, where in ye shall see strange things ... God's smock, Our Lady's smock, part of God's supper on the Lord's table, part of the stone of the manger in which was born Jesus in Bethlehem; belike there is in Bethlehem plenty of stones and some quarry ... all this of Maiden Bradley, where is an holy father prior and hath but 6 children ... His sons be tall men waiting upon him, and he thanks God he never meddled with married women, but all with maidens the fairest could be got, and always married them right well. The pope considering his fragility, gave him licence to keep a whore ...

Letter from Dr. Richard Layton, Commissioner to Cromwell, 1535.

  Can you find aspects of this priest's life which seem to go against the teaching of the church?

CORE ACTIVITIES

1 Read the letters sent to Cromwell.
 * What type of information were Cromwell's commissioners looking for?
 * What examples can you find in these extracts about the kindness, consideration and fairness of the commissioners?
 * Why do you think they showed such concern if their task was to close down all the religious houses?

A EARL OF ESSEX.

Thomas Cromwell.

Evidence

C

We have ... left the canons and monks still in their houses, without any clear discharge of them, but have put them at their liberty and choice ... to go ... to their friends ... the most part desire to have capacities (livings) and some to be assigned over to other places of religion ...
The house of Dover is a goodly house and well repaired ...
The house of Folkestone is a little house, well repaired, and the prior is a very honest person ... beloved amongst his neighbours.

Letter from Kent Commissioners to Cromwell, November 1535.

D

I write to you in favour of the house of Woolstrope (Lincolnshire) the governor ... is well beloved, having eight religious persons being priests of right good conversation and living religiously, having such qualities of virtue as we have not found the like in no place; they can and doth use either embroidering, writing books with very fair hand, making their own garments, carving, painting or engraving ... pity alone causeth me to write.

Letter from George Giffard, Commissioner to Cromwell, June 1536.

 Which parts of **B** and **C** helped Cromwell to justify the royal policy to close monasteries?

Giffard may have been anxious to stress his own honesty. When he wrote on behalf of another house not being closed, the king had accused him of accepting bribes.

Fearing the commissioners visit meant closure, some abbots quickly sold off their lands, hid their treasures or even armed their monks.

E

The poor people thoroughly in every place be so greedy upon these houses when they be suppressed, that by night and day, not only of the towns but also of the country, they do continually resort as long as any door, window, iron or glass, or loose lead remaineth in any of them.

John London, Commissioner to Cromwell, November 1538.

 What evidence in **D** and **E** would not have pleased Cromwell?

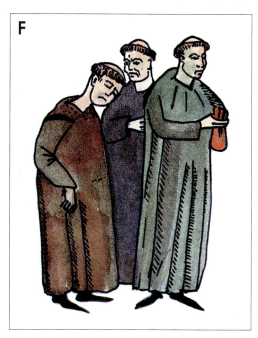

Victims of the dissolution.

2 Look at **D**.
 • Are these tasks what you might expect from monks in a small house?

3 Look at **E**.
 • What methods might the commissioners have considered to solve the problem of looting the suppressed houses?

EXTENSION ACTIVITY

1 **B**, **C**, **D** and **E** come from a collection of reports sent to Cromwell.
 • What conclusions can you draw about:
  - the attitude of Cromwell's commissioners?
  - the value of this collection in providing evidence of the state of the monasteries at this time?

6. EDWARD VI AND MARY TUDOR

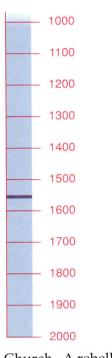

Targets

* To examine the rapid changes in government and religion.
* To identify aspects of continuity which influenced the course of events.

1547 - 1553:
The Reign of Edward VI

The new king was an intelligent and thoughtful boy of nine. His uncle, the Duke of Somerset, became Protector (adviser to the king and in charge of the kingdom). He introduced the English Prayer Book, written by Thomas Cranmer, which gave a clear Protestant doctrine for the Church. A rebellion in favour of the Catholic mass (form of service) was suppressed in Cornwall and Devon. The Protector also seized the remaining property of the Church, setting up King Edward VI Grammar Schools with some of the profits. For himself, he built a fine palace, Somerset House, by the Thames.

The most serious uprising was in Norfolk led by Robert Ket. The causes were economic: rising prices and the over-grazing of common land. Somerset felt some sympathy for the rebels. When he failed to act quickly, a rival faction led by the Duke of Northumberland seized power.

Churches were stripped of any remaining images, and gold and silver plate, and their walls were whitewashed. Altars were replaced by communion tables. Of course the profits again found their way into the pockets of the ruling faction at court.

All the duke's plans were upset by Edward's illness in 1553. He persuaded the king to leave the throne to his own daughter-in-law, Lady Jane Grey. However, Henry VIII's two daughters, Mary and Elizabeth, had the greater claim. Most people thought so too; when Edward died, they flocked to Mary's side and Jane and her supporters faced the inevitable death at the block.

Henry VIII had faced some opposition to his takeover of the Church. The most serious uprising, the 'Pilgrimage of Grace' in the north in 1536, was ruthlessly put down. An English Bible was placed in every church but the form of religion remained fairly Catholic. However, as if he realised the direction for the future, Henry allowed his only son, Edward, to be educated by protestant tutors.

Edward VI.

CORE ACTIVITIES

1 This period saw three serious rebellions.
 ● What was the main cause of each?
 ● What does this indicate about popular feeling on religious issues?

2 Despite all the ups and downs of these two reigns, sometimes events were influenced by attitudes which had not changed.
 ● Can you find any examples?

Change and Continuity

1553 - 1558:
The Reign of Mary Tudor

The daughter of Catherine of Aragon had remained a firm Catholic during the upheavals of her father's reign. Now as a mature woman she restored the Catholic Church and married Philip, the heir to the Spanish throne. A son would have been heir to both kingdoms. Many English people objected to this prospect, even though they were happy to be Catholics again. A rebellion to prevent the marriage, led by Sir Thomas Wyatt, was only just defeated. As a precaution Mary imprisoned her sister, Elizabeth, in the Tower.

Philip.

Mary Tudor.

 What sort of person does Mary seem to be?

Mary is best remembered for her fierce hatred of all Protestants. About 300 were burnt to death, including former church leaders Cranmer, Hooper, Latimer and Ridley, as well as many ordinary people. The Catholic religion became associated in English minds with persecution and foreign influence.

The queen's life turned into tragedy when Philip dragged her country into a war between France and Spain. It led to the loss of England's last continental foothold at Calais.

Mary rarely saw Philip yet had pathetic hopes for the child which would have ensured the survival of Catholicism as the established religion in England. She died of a tumour, hastened by the influenza which was sweeping the country in a severe epidemic.

Conclusions

Historians tend to see these two reigns as a period when England was suffering in a variety of ways. Henry VIII had spent most of his wealth from the Reformation on futile wars against France. Under Edward the crown was dominated by greedy nobles. The image of 'Bloody Mary' was confirmed by Foxe's 'Book of Martyrs', published in 1563, which was immensely popular and turned her victims into national heroes and heroines. These years also saw bad harvests and debasements (reductions in value) of the coinage. According to one modern calculation, the cost of living doubled between 1549 and 1557. Prices generally only rose by 50% during the whole of Henry VIII's reign.

EXTENSION ACTIVITY

1 One historian has suggested that if either of these two monarchs had lived another ten years, the history of England would have been very different.
 - Can you suggest why this comment was made?
 - Discuss your ideas in a small group.

7. THE YOUNG QUEEN ELIZABETH

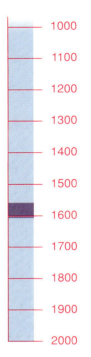

Target

* To investigate the problems Elizabeth faced in 1558 and how she made key decisions about her country's future.

Elizabeth was 25 when she became queen in 1558. She was the daughter of Henry VIII and Anne Boleyn. Her mother had been executed and her own life had been in danger when her sister Mary had imprisoned her briefly in the Tower of London.

To survive as the ruler she had to find ways of keeping the loyalty of her subjects and defending her country against foreign invaders. If we look at the situation she faced at this time we may be able to decide whether Elizabeth made the right decisions or whether she survived more by good luck than judgement.

One way to decide what to do when you are faced with a problem is to try to avoid the mistakes which other people have made. We may be able to understand the decisions Elizabeth took if we look at what went wrong under Edward and Mary.

At first Elizabeth had two very close advisers. William Cecil, at 38, was the youngest member of the royal council. He had been Principal Secretary under Edward. Now he took up the same post again. Robert Dudley, son of the Duke of Northumberland, was a handsome young courtier. Elizabeth was very fond of him. His wife, Amy, was found dead at the foot of a staircase in 1560. Some of the queen's enemies suggested she had been murdered to leave Dudley free to marry Elizabeth. Cecil and Dudley became leaders of rival factions at court. However, Elizabeth always had the last word on any important decisions and never let anyone else run her government.

Elizabeth at her coronation.

Can you identify the objects which suggest that this was Elizabeth's coronation?

B

The Queen poor, the realm exhausted, the nobility poor and decayed ... The people out of order. Justice not executed. All things dear ... Divisions amongst ourselves. Wars with France and Scotland.

A description of England in 1558 by one of the queen's advisers.

What sort of land had Elizabeth inherited?

CORE ACTIVITY

1 Try answering these questions without looking back in the book.
- Who were the real rulers during Edward VI's reign?
- What policies brought rebellions against the government?
- What decisions did Mary take which made her unpopular?
- What conclusions could Elizabeth draw from these facts?

Viewpoints

The most urgent decision Elizabeth faced was over religion. Her father had angered Catholics by replacing the Pope as head of the English Church and allowing English bibles to be used. Her brother had encouraged more extreme Protestants and her sister had restored the Catholic Church.

Elizabeth's own religious beliefs were unclear. She was educated as a Protestant but liked Catholic ornaments in her private chapel. At her coronation she disappeared behind a screen when the bishop said a mass in Latin.

William Cecil.

Robert Dudley, Earl of Leicester.

ELIZABETH'S THREE CHOICES IN RELIGION

FOR	AGAINST
▼ **She could keep England Catholic.**	
Spain would remain friendly. The French would not risk an invasion. Elizabeth would have to do nothing.	Elizabeth would lose control of and revenue from the English Church. She might be under the influence of Spain and become associated with her sister's unpopular persecution of protestants. Many gentlemen who had gained land from the church might rebel rather than give it back.
▼ **She could make England completely Protestant.**	
Spain, France and the Pope would be her enemies.	It would please many subjects who hated Mary's persecution and foreign influence.
▼ **She could find a middle way between the two.**	
This would please a growing number of her subjects who had grown used to an English church and some Protestant ceremonies and ideas.	It would not satisfy foreign Catholic powers. Extreme Protestants in England would be angry and might stir up unrest.

EXTENSION ACTIVITY

1 Think about Elizabeth's religious beliefs.
   - What decision should Elizabeth have made over religion? Discuss this in a small group and compare your decision with the others in your class.
   - Make a list of the problems which Elizabeth faced at the start of her reign.
   - Can you think of any advantages Elizabeth had which might have helped her to become a more effective ruler than her brother or sister?

   (See page 63 for Elizabeth's decision.)

8. ELIZABETH AND MARY

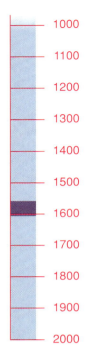

Targets

* To examine the problem of Elizabeth's succession.
* To investigate her treatment of her cousin, Mary.

Elizabeth and Mary, Queen of Scotland, never met but their lives were linked by royal blood. Mary was next in line to the English throne. For many years she was a symbol of hope for those who wanted to see the Catholic religion restored in England.

In 1562 Elizabeth nearly died from smallpox. She was careful not to name her legal heir.

Elizabeth seriously considered marriage. Several foreign royal suitors tried to win her hand. By playing them along, the queen at least kept their friendship. However, time was not on her side. As the chances of her ever having a child receded, the threat from Mary seemed to grow. English Protestants believed that only Elizabeth's life stood between them and another persecution by a Catholic queen.

Mary was tall, beautiful, with dark eyes and a fair skin. She won the admiration of the French court as the wife of Francis II. After her husband's death in 1560, she returned to Scotland.

For ten years Elizabeth's policy of doing nothing about marriage and her succession worked. Then in the spring of 1568 Mary appeared in England seeking help and refuge. She had lost popularity in Scotland after a series of quarrels with Protestant nobles and two unfortunate marriages. Elizabeth had nothing to gain by sending her back. She kept Mary in prison for 18 years.

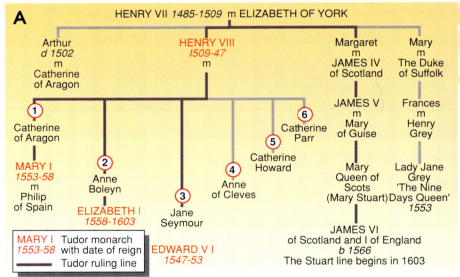

Tudor Family Tree.

B

'When my sister Mary was Queen, what prayers were made by many to see me placed in her seat ... Now then, if the affections of our people grow faint ... what may we look for when evil-minded men shall have a foreign prince appointed the certain successor to the crown? In how great danger shall I be ...'

Queen Elizabeth's message to the House of Commons, 1559.

 What do you think this message means?

During this time civil war between Protestants and Catholics raged in France and the Netherlands, which were part of Philip of Spain's empire. Elizabeth sent help to the Dutch rebels. Not surprisingly, Spanish agents organised plots against her life. In 1570 the Catholic Duke of Norfolk was drawn into a plan to marry Mary and help her gain the throne. Though he was found guilty of treason, Elizabeth resisted demands for his execution. Eventually she gave in, partly to save Mary from the same fate.

English Catholics had to choose between loyalty to their queen or the Pope when he excommunicated Elizabeth.

Role of the individual

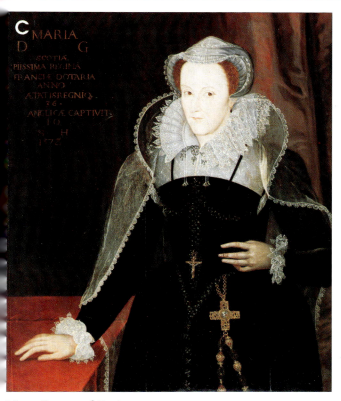

C

Mary Queen of Scots.

Their priests hid in specially constructed 'holes' in manor houses. The government suspected leading Catholics of conspiracy. Mary continued to lend her support to plots.

In 1586 she was found guilty of treason. Still Elizabeth hesitated, signing but refusing to send the death warrant to Fotheringay Castle. Finally, in February 1587, Mary was beheaded. Elizabeth was distraught and even tried to deny responsibility for putting her royal cousin to death.

CORE ACTIVITIES

1 Think carefully about Elizabeth's actions.
  - Why did Elizabeth refuse to name her successor?

2 Many gave support to Catholic plots after Elizabeth had been excommunicated.
  - Why did Elizabeth allow Mary to remain in England in 1568?

3 Some historians have said that Elizabeth had to execute Mary sooner or later in order to keep her throne.
  - Do you agree?
  - Explain your answer.

D

This cruel act must be the last of many which she of England has performed and that of our Lord will be served if she receives the punishment she deserved for so many years.

The Duke of Parma in a letter to Philip of Spain, 1587.

? *Why might Spain be against the execution of Mary?*

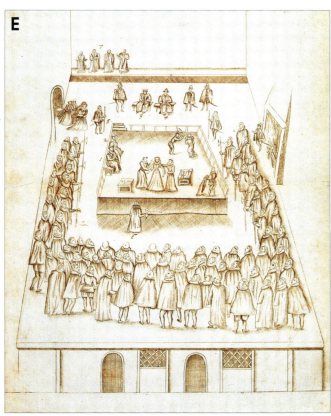

The execution of Mary.

EXTENSION ACTIVITY

1 The two queens seem to have been trapped by circumstances into a deadly rivalry.
  - Was this really the case?
  - Can you think of anything they had in common which could have brought them closer?
  - Discuss this in a small group and make a list of your conclusions for a wall display.

9. THE SPANISH ARMADA OF 1588

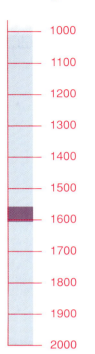

Targets

* To investigate the reasons for the launch and defeat of the Armada.
* To examine the significance of the event in history.

The most dramatic moments in any nation's history occur when it is threatened with invasion by a foreign power. We have seen how in 1066 the Norman conquest changed the course of English history. In 1588 and 1940 similar invasions were imminent but on both occasions the defenders won the day.

The execution of Mary made Philip of Spain determined to invade England. He believed that Mary had bequeathed him her claim to the throne. As champion of the Catholics he said that he had a holy mission to overthrow the Protestant, Elizabeth.

Philip had been king of both Spain and Portugal since 1580. With the vast wealth and shipping of both countries he was able to mount a great expedition against England. There were also very practical reasons to attack the country which was supporting Dutch rebels against Spanish rule and sending its 'sea dogs' like Francis Drake and John Hawkins to capture and plunder the Spanish treasure ships en route from America.

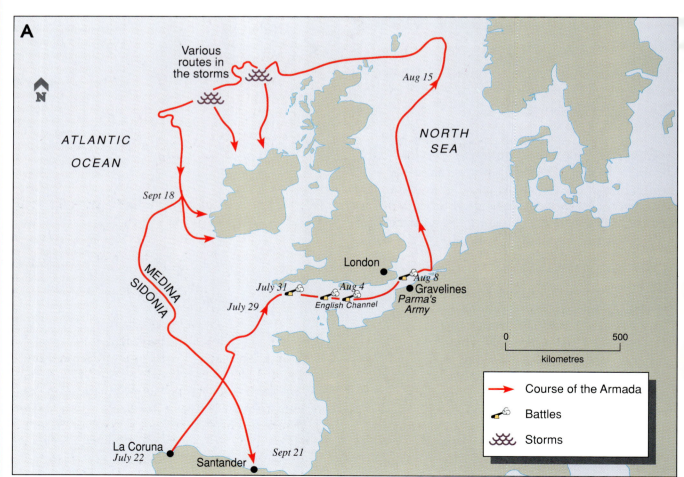

The Route of the Spanish Armada.

Causation and Motivation

The Spanish Grand Fleet or Armada set sail under the command of the Duke of Medina Sidonia in the summer of 1588. The main part of the English navy was based at Plymouth. Lord Howard of Effingham was in charge; the most famous Elizabethan seamen, Drake, Hawkins and Martin Frobisher, commanded squadrons.

B

Sir Francis Drake, pictured in 1581, when he was knighted for sailing around the world and bringing riches for the queen plundered from Spanish ships and colonies.

Drake had shown his skill by sinking or capturing 37 ships at the Spanish port of Cadiz in April 1587, delaying the Armada for a year. He declared 'I have singed the King of Spain's beard.'

The English Fleet

A total of 197 ships
34 war galleons
30 146 tonnes
Just over 15 000 men

The vessels were little different in size but the English warships included several re-designed by Hawkins. These could outsail and outmanoeuvre the Spanish and were fitted with accurate and powerful guns. Sidonia wrote: ' ... their ships are so fast and so nimble, they can do anything they like with them.'

The Spanish Armada

A total of 128 ships
24 war galleons
58 408 tonnes
Almost 30 000 men

The Spanish reached the English Channel on Friday, July 29. Two days later the Mayor and people of Plymouth had a grandstand view of the first skirmish between the fleets. Many sailed out in small boats to get a closer look or even try to help in the fight. But the English cannon could not disturb the tight crescent formation of the Armada as it sailed past the Isle of Wight towards Calais.

Causation and Motivation

The Plan

The Spanish plan was to reach the Dutch coast and transport an army based there across to England. However, small Dutch boats patrolled the coastline and prevented the Spanish troops' barges rowing out to the fleet. When the Armada anchored off Calais on August 8th, a swift current carried eight fireships, covered with pitch, oil and tar, into the midst of the Spanish formation. The captains quickly cut their cables and set sail. All the next day in rough seas the dispersed galleons were attacked by the English in the battle of Gravelines. Damaged and short of ammunition, Sidonia's fleet was in no fit state to return to Calais. His remaining ships sailed north in an attempt to return home via the north of Scotland. Many were wrecked on the shores of western Ireland. Those who did not drown were murdered by Elizabeth's soldiers. In the whole expedition 65 ships were lost; 20 000 men died, half through sickness and starvation. By comparison no English ships were lost and fewer than 100 men died in battle. However, about 7 000 perished from disease during the campaign.

Spanish and English galleons.

The Verdict

Some historians describe the event as a victory for the smaller, quicker English ships against the large, cumbersome Spanish galleons. Others claim that the defeat was the result of a freak storm which scattered the Spanish ships and drove them into the North Sea, rather than the courage and skill of English seamen. This view is endorsed by the commemorative medal which was struck on Elizabeth's orders; it stated 'God blew and they were scattered'.

CORE ACTIVITIES

1 Using the information in this unit:
- Make a list of as many dates as you can, between April 1587 and September 1588.
- Now use these dates to draw a timeline of the Armada.

2 Look at **C**.
- How evenly matched were the Spanish and English fleets?
- Can you suggest any other advantages which the English might have had?

3 Think about the information you have looked at in this unit.
- What conclusions can you draw about naval warfare and the conditions on board ship at this time?

EXTENSION ACTIVITY

1 Think about the Armada campaign.
- Discuss what were the crucial moments.
- Suggest why historians have presented different versions of the event.

10. THE RISE OF THE GENTRY

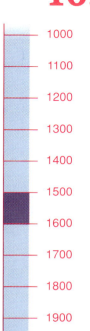

Targets

* To investigate the economic and social changes.
* To consider how the increasing number of landowners affected the Crown and nobility.

In 1485 the population of England and Wales was about 2 million. In 1603 when Elizabeth I died, it stood at 4 million in England and approximately 300 000 in Wales.

The largest city in Europe dominated English life. 'Soon London will be all England' complained James I. Feeding and ruling its 200 000 people was a major problem for the Crown and the City Council.

Regional centres such as Bristol, Norwich and York had populations of about 12 000 while other towns were much smaller. Although their leading citizens had power as councillors and JPs, they tended to look to nobles at court for support on any matter. For example, the Earl of Leicester was High Steward of Bristol even though he rarely visited the city.

90% of the population lived by farming. When a farmer died his land would usually be divided between his sons and their families. This meant that more people had to live off the same amount of land. Often a younger son had to move elsewhere or enter the Church.

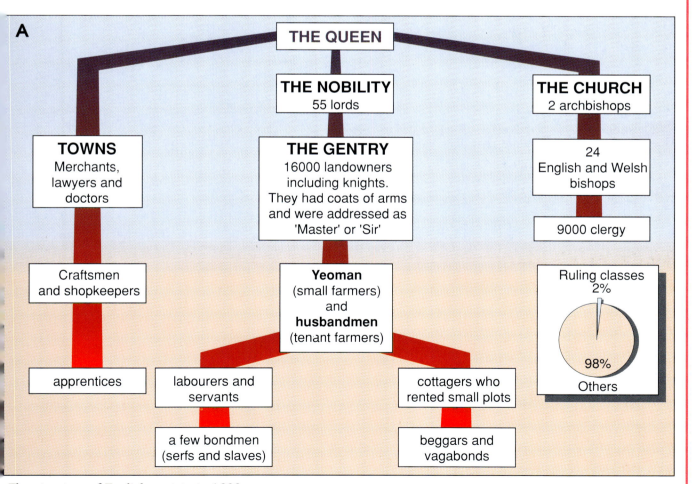

The structure of English society in 1600.

Change and Continuity

Prices and Wages

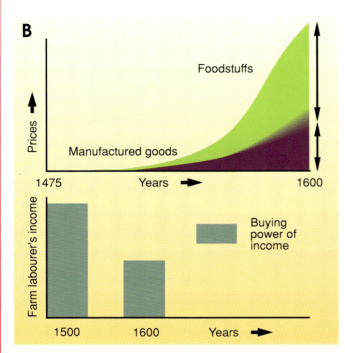

Wages lagged behind prices so that a typical farm labourer's income fell by over 50% during the 16th century in terms of buying power.

Although it was slow by comparison with the late 20th century, such inflation of prices seemed alarming to people in Tudor times. The rise began in the 1520s when Henry VIII raised taxes and debased the coinage to pay for war against France. This recurred in the 1540s when the sale of most of the land confiscated during the Reformation and another debasement still failed to meet the cost of wars.

The Crown could only just manage to meet its daily expenses in peacetime. Any additional costs meant new taxes, land sales or loans.

Although a growing population increased the demand for food, many landowners found that producing sheep for wool was more profitable. Enclosure of arable land, including the removal of tenants, occurred in the Midlands, despite laws against it. Cloth exports from London doubled during the first half of the 16th century.

The influx of silver from the New World, brought by Spanish treasure galleons, was another reason for price rises across Europe.

The Rise of the Gentry

In any period some families grow rich while others decline. Such changes within society are called 'social mobility'. It is easy to see why the prosperity of landowners, some from humble origins, grew as demand for food and wool increased. Instead of a pattern of lords and tenants in most villages, these independent farmers were a kind of middle group, gaining influence in their local areas as employers and JPs. As a group they wanted a share of power at court and in Parliament. In towns, merchants, lawyers and doctors were also prospering. Some invested in land and built country houses themselves. The Crown and aristocracy had to come to terms with this new phenomenon. If they decided not to share power, some of the gentry might try to seize it and that could mean civil war.

C

Well, I say it was never merry world in England since gentlemen came up.
Of course by a somewhat unusual route, Shakespeare, the son of a tradesman, rose to become a gentleman with his own coat of arms.

Henry VI. Shakespeare.

 What do you think this comment might mean?

All this meant little for the role of women in society. Sometimes the gentry married into noble families. Marriages were often arranged like property deals. In the lower classes it was not unusual for a man to sell a wife he was tired of at the local hiring fair.

D

... those whom nature hath made to keepe home and to nourish their familie and children, and not to medle with matters abroade, not to beare office in a citie or common wealth no more than children and infantes.

De Republica Anglorum. Sir Thomas Smith, 1565.

 Describe to a friend what you think this source means.

Change and Continuity

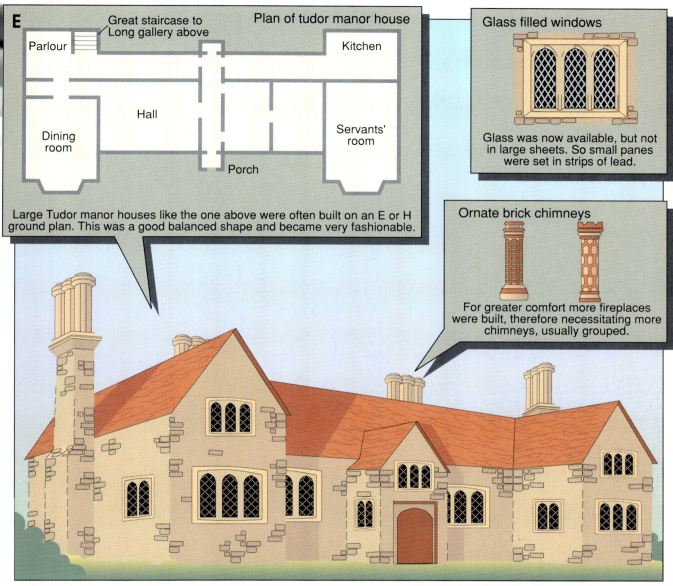

An Elizabethan country house.

CORE ACTIVITIES

1 Using the information in this unit, answer the following questions.
- How did the rise in population affect food prices and land shortages?
- What changes encouraged the gentry to become landowners?
- Why was London so important in the national economy?

2 Look at **E**.
- What type of person was most likely to have owned a house like this? *(CLUE TO SUCCESS: Read the section The Rise of the Gentry)*

EXTENSION ACTIVITIES

1 **C** is from a play about events in the mid-15th century.
- How can it be useful for attitudes a century later?

2 Sum up the attitude expressed in **D**.
- How would you explain this point of view given the fact that a woman was the monarch at this time?

3 Historians have different views about the rise of the gentry in this century.
- In a small group, discuss the evidence for and against the suggestion.
- Record your conclusions.

11. THE GUNPOWDER PLOT

Targets

* To investigate the causes and results of the Plot.
* To examine the suggestion that the government encouraged it.

When Elizabeth died in 1603 the crown passed to James Stuart, the son of Mary Queen of Scots. He was already king of Scotland but despite having the same monarch, the two countries continued to be governed separately.

The Gunpowder Plotters.

James was a Protestant but felt that Catholics should be left free to worship. However, his chief adviser and secretary, Robert Cecil, warned that this would leave them free to plot to kill him in order to place a Catholic on the throne. So James agreed to enforce harsh laws to punish English Catholics and drive out their priests.

The Anglo-Spanish Conference in London, 1604. This meeting ended the war with Spain. Robert Cecil is the figure on the right hand side.

Causation and Motivation

The Gunpowder Plot was planned by Robert Catesby who persuaded two Yorkshire Catholics, Francis Tresham and Thomas Percy, to help him to blow up the king and his supporters during the opening of Parliament on November 5th, 1605. This was to be followed by an armed rising in the Midlands. At first they tried tunnelling from a nearby house. This proved difficult but in May they were able to rent the room beneath Parliament itself. Over 1 ton of gunpowder barrels were placed under firewood and coal. A Catholic from York, Guido Fawkes, agreed to hide there and keep watch.

C

... let his Majesty know that I dare boldly say no shower nor storm shall mar our harvest, except it should come from the middle region.

An extract from a letter written by Cecil to another courtier on October 24th, 1605.

 Can you explain the meaning of this sentence? (CLUE TO SUCCESS: How would letting the plot develop help Cecil to catch the leaders?)

Robert Cecil had spies watching such leading Catholics. It seems probable that he knew about the Plot at an early stage from his friend, Lord Mounteagle, the brother in law of Francis Tresham.

On the evening of October 26th a stranger delivered an anonymous letter to Lord Mounteagle. It included this warning: '... devise some excuse to shift your attendance at this parliament ... I say they shall receive a terrible blow this parliament and yet they shall not see who hurts them.'

The letter was passed to Cecil who showed it to the king. Soon after midnight on November 5th Guy Fawkes was arrested in the cellar, with matches in his possession. Great publicity was given to the discovery and the other leading conspirators were tracked down to a house in Staffordshire where Catesby and Percy were shot dead. Fawkes was tortured and executed along with other captured plotters in January 1606.

James I, 1566 - 1625.

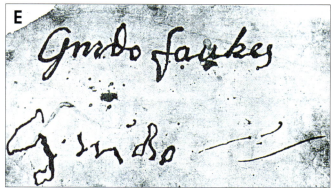

Guy Fawkes' signatures before and after torture.

 Why are they so different?

Causation and Motivation

The anonymous letter sent to Lord Mounteagle.

The Mystery of Francis Tresham
He was captured and put in the Tower of London. He became seriously ill and died in great pain on December 23rd. A post mortem revealed poison. It has been suggested that he was the author of the Mounteagle letter. Cecil had him killed before he could reveal this fact at his trial. Alternatively he may have poisoned himself in the hope that his death before conviction for treason would mean that his property could be passed on to his family. Otherwise it would be confiscated by the king.

The Results of the Plot
More severe laws were passed against Catholics who could not become doctors, lawyers or civil servants. There were no more plots against James's life and he was free to concentrate on trying to raise money and rule without interference from Parliament. Many MPs had other ideas; they wanted a greater share in making policy, to keep taxes down and help the cause of Protestantism abroad. These disagreements between the Crown and Parliament grew more serious as time went on.

CORE ACTIVITY

1 Read these pages carefully then answer these questions.
- What were the aims of the leaders of the Gunpowder Plot?
- What clues are there in **F** to suggest the letter was a forgery?
- Who had a motive for forging the letter?

EXTENSION ACTIVITY

1 Let us assume that Robert Cecil knew of the plot and encouraged it.
- What evidence can you find to show his influence on the course of events?
- In a small group, prepare the script for a discussion between two historians. One believes that Robert Cecil played a leading part in encouraging the plot; the other argues that this was too risky and the whole course of events can be explained by a straightforward conspiracy by these Catholics.
- You could tape the discussion and end with an explanation about why the event is still commemorated on each Bonfire Night.

12. THE LIFE OF THE POOR

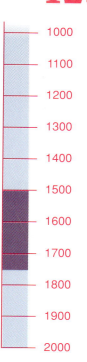

Target

* To compare attitudes during 1500 - 1750 with those of today.

Tudor Times

It seems likely that since the earliest times there have always been people who were poorer than others. However, it was during the reign of Elizabeth I that the poor became a real problem.

Some of these poor people roamed from village to village, turning to crime to survive. There were several reasons for this.
- Methods of farming began to change. Fields were enclosed. Fewer crops were grown and more people kept sheep.
- Monasteries were closed (see Unit 5).
- The population began to grow.
- There were fewer wars so fewer men were needed in the army and navy.

Treatment of the poor from a contemporary engraving.

How are the beggars being punished in this engraving?

B

Ann Buckle of the age of 46 years, widow ... hath 2 children, the one of the age of 9 and the other of 5 years that work lace, and hath dwelt here ever - no alms (money given to poor) but very poor.

John Findley, of the age of 82 years, cooper (barrel maker) not in work, and Joan his wife, sickly that spin and knit, and hath dwelt here ever ...

From the 1570 census of Norwich.

What do you think the words 'hath dwelt here ever' might mean?

Solving the Problem

Many of the rich people thought the poor were lazy and therefore should be punished. However, the Church had always taught that the poor should be cared for. Also books, like Thomas More's *Utopia*, criticised riches. Eventually, Elizabeth's last Parliament passed a Poor Law which was very different from those of previous Parliaments.

C

Be it enacted, that the churchwardens of every parish and four well-off house-owners ... shall be called overseers of the poor ... They shall ... set to work the children of all parents who shall not ... be thought able to keep and support their children, and also all persons who, married or unmarried, having no means to maintain them, use no ordinary and daily trade of like to get their living by ...

An extract from the 1601 Poor Law.

Which two groups of people does this part of the Act mention?

31

Similarity and Difference

The money for the poor was to be raised from a special tax called a 'rate'. Materials were to be provided for those fit to work, but anyone who refused this offer of work was to be sent to prison. This Poor Law lasted over 230 years.

Stuart Times

Despite the Poor Law, there were still many poor people during the reign of the Stuarts. Ordinary people continued to live in houses which were tiny, cramped and dirty. Often if people got into debt their only option was to run away.

Beggars in Stuart times.

Why do you think these people are having to beg?

E

After some years of this Samuel Downton and his wife ran away from Cockshutt in the night time and left all their children behind them - four of which were afterwards paid for by the parish of Ellesmere. They went into Staffordshire. There he went a-begging like an old broken down person and she carried a box with pins and laces.

An account from 1700.

What do you think 'paid for by the Parish of Ellesmere' might mean?

The 18th Century

Remember that the number of poor people in Tudor times grew because landowners started enclosing their fields with hedges. This meant that people who had relied on the land for a living began to move into the towns. There it was often difficult to find work. Many employers kept wages low because they thought that if wages went up the poor would not want to work for as many hours. This may have been because poor people were expected to work between 16 and 18 hours every day.

Many parishes built workhouses where poor people were sent to live. From here they were hired out to employers. Conditions in these workhouses were dreadful and people hated being sent there.

Conclusion

Because almost all poor people were unable to read and write we have very little to tell us whether they resented such low wages and their lack of freedom. Perhaps they simply accepted it or thought that this was how God intended life to be. Later in the 19th century we will see how the poor and ordinary people began to make demands for more freedom.

CORE ACTIVITY

1 Using the information in this unit and your own knowledge of life today do the following.
- Write a short report about how poor people were treated during the period 1500 - 1750.
- Write a short report about how poor people are treated today.
- Now write a final paragraph or draw a series of illustrations to show any differences you can find between the attitude towards the poor today, compared with the attitude towards the poor during 1500 -1750. *(CLUE TO SUCCESS:* You may need to talk with your teacher about the meaning of the word attitude*)*

EXTENSION ACTIVITIES

1 Working with a small group of friends:
- Write a short play about the lives of rich people (see Unit 11) and the lives of the poor during the period 1500 - 1750.
- Try to show how their lives were different.

2 Using this book and any others which are available to you find out more about the punishments which the poor had to endure. You could write and record a short radio programme about your findings and then play it to your group or class.

13. CHARLES I

Targets

* To investigate the causes of the Civil War.
* To consider how far Charles I was responsible.

Born in 1600, Charles spent his early years trying to copy his athletic and handsome elder brother, Henry. Charles suffered from weak leg joints, a speech impediment and shyness. Henry told him to be a bishop since the gown would hide his legs! Indeed, this might have suited such a sensitive and deeply religious character.

In 1612 Henry died from typhoid. James I's favourite, George Villiers, Duke of Buckingham, became Charles's new friend and mentor. This charming and ambitious homosexual was the virtual ruler of England until he was murdered by a sailor at Portsmouth in 1628. By that time Charles was facing the problems which were to lead to civil war.

Charles I.

Why did war break out between Charles and Parliament?

Serious arguments often begin over trivial matters. There are usually deep seated reasons for wars which the words of politicians reflect and make worse. If we look at the beliefs and ambitions of each side, these basic reasons may become clear.

THE KING	PARLIAMENT
POLITICS	
Charles believed in divine right and his sole control over foreign policy. Most of the 122 peers and other nobles naturally supported the hereditary monarchy.	The Commons wanted more control of policy by limiting the money supply to the government. The protection of the interests of wealthy farmers and merchants, rather than ideas of liberty or democracy, lay behind these aims.
FINANCE	
Charles had income from crown land, customs duties and the sale of titles. Fines on landowners for enclosing and breaking medieval forest laws made him unpopular. In 1635 he imposed 'ship money', a tax to pay for the navy, on all areas instead of only ports.	Parliament refused to grant the king the normal right to collect customs duties throughout his reign. It also opposed forced loans and the sale of monopolies to merchants who wanted the sole right to make or sell particular goods.
RELIGION	
Charles was a devout Anglican and encouraged William Laud, Archbishop of Canterbury, to make churches more beautiful with pictures and images. Clergy should wear vestments and the communion table must be railed off from the congregation.	Since Elizabeth's reign, Puritans had become more powerful in the House of Commons. They demanded reforms making services simpler and making each church virtually independent, under the control of its minister and his congregation.

Causation

For 11 years, from 1629, Charles ruled without calling Parliament. Some of the leading MPs were arrested. Every source of money was exploited. Charles borrowed heavily from merchants. However, he became increasingly unpopular. In 1640 he was forced to recall Parliament when his religious policy provoked a civil war in Scotland.

The 'Long Parliament' was to sit for the next 20 years. It forced the king to sacrifice his leading adviser, the Earl of Strafford, who was beheaded for 'high treason'. The royal courts of Star Chamber and the Council of the North were abolished along with Laud's own Court of High Commission. As the speed of change increased some MPs became concerned about how far the shift in power would go. Many people felt more secure with the form of government they knew. The radical leaders in Parliament were as fanatical about their beliefs as Charles and Laud were about divine right and a Church ruled by bishops. Rather than go to the other extreme, many MPs decided to support the king.

In November 1641 Parliament narrowly passed the 'Grand Remonstrance' which stated that MPs should choose the king's councillors and reform the Church. The king's angry response was to demand the arrest of the 'Five Members' who led the Commons. He took armed men into the House but found that 'all the birds are flown'. This rash action made war between king and Parliament inevitable.

It was at this moment that the two nicknames associated with the Civil War appeared. The Royalists called the tough close cropped apprentices who rioted against the king 'Roundheads'. The king's men were called 'Cavaliers' after the Spanish soldiers, the 'cavalieros' who were suppressing Protestants in Europe.

Puritans wore plain black and white dress. This was in sharp contrast to the colourful and flamboyant clothes worn by the king and his rich supporters.

CORE ACTIVITIES

1 Using the information in this unit:
 • List all the reasons for the war between Charles I and Parliament.

2 Historians have many different opinions on the origins of the civil war.
 • Using the evidence in this unit, try to give your views on:
  - how far Charles himself was to blame
  - how far the situation generally made war certain

EXTENSION ACTIVITY

1 It has been suggested that anyone who studies this period soon takes sides.
 • In the crisis of 1641 would you have been a Cavalier or a Roundhead?
 • Give your reasons and try to justify these in a small group discussion.

14. THE ENGLISH CIVIL WAR

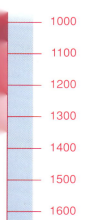

Targets

* To investigate the course of the Civil War.
* To examine how this sequence explains the fate of Charles I.

In 1642 most English people did not want to destroy the monarchy. Seven years later the king was executed and England was declared to be a 'Commonwealth' or republic. Of course in wars feelings and attitudes are very extreme; how else can you bring yourself to kill your enemy? Was death the inevitable price Charles had to pay for losing the war? If not, can we find any other reason in the course of events?

England in 1642.

1642
July: The king raised his standard at Nottingham. His chief support came from the nobility, Anglicans, landowners and the north and west of England. He possessed the better cavalry, commanded by his nephew, Prince Rupert. Parliament controlled the navy, the better infantry and London.

October: The first major battle at Edgehill was indecisive. Charles pressed on to attack London but retreated in the face of Parliament's larger army.

1643
There were victories for both sides but the king failed to break through to threaten London. Parliament's alliance with the Scots brought a fresh danger to Charles from the north. The Parliamentary army was reorganised. Oliver Cromwell, a squire from Huntingdon, emerged as a cavalry commander to rival Rupert.

A pikeman and an infantry officer in the Royalist army.

? What sort of problems might have arisen when fighting with these weapons?

1644
July: Sir Thomas Fairfax led the combined armies of Parliament and Scotland to a crushing victory over the royalists at Marston Moor in Yorkshire. The king had lost control of the north.

35

Chronology

1645
Negotiations with the king failed. Cromwell urged a quick end to the war by organising the New Model Army. This regularly paid professional force destroyed the last Royalist army at Naseby in June. The king even lost his private papers which showed he was trying to gain help from France by promising concessions to Catholics.

1646
April: Charles surrendered to the Scots. He hoped that divisions among the victors could be turned to his own advantage. The Presbyterians who controlled Parliament and London wanted a national church without bishops, run by small assemblies. The Independents who dominated the army wanted each congregation to govern itself or, in practice, accept the wishes of the leaders in the local community.

1647
January: The Scots sold Charles to Parliament for £400 000. It tried to disband the New Model Army but instead Cromwell and Fairfax occupied London. Debates between political factions at Putney Church showed that deep differences remained. In November, Charles escaped to Carisbrooke Castle on the Isle of Wight. He made a treaty with the Scottish Presbyterians.

Prince Rupert.

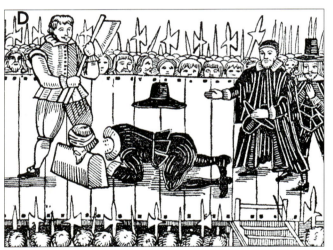

On a scaffold outside the Banqueting Hall in Whitehall, on a chilly morning, Charles showed great dignity as he met his fate. He was seen as a martyr by some.

1648
The Scots invaded England and a naval mutiny gave Charles many ships. This second civil war quickly ended with victory over the Scots at Preston. Cromwell and his commanders saw no point in further talks with a king who always plotted behind their backs. Now they were determined to punish him. In December, Colonel Pride expelled the Presbyterians from Parliament leaving 100 Independents (the Rump) to set up a court to try the king.

1649
The trial at Westminster Hall was brief. Charles refused to recognise the court as legal but he was sentenced to death because he had 'traitorously and maliciously levied war against the present Parliament and the people therein represented'. On January 30th, Charles was executed. For Cromwell and the army, his removal was essential. The monarchy and the House of Lords were quickly abolished by the Rump.

CORE ACTIVITIES

1 Devise a timeline from 1642 - 1649.
  • Place all these events their correct place.

2 Three key events probably led to Charles' defeat in the Civil War of 1642-46.
  • Can you identify these?
  • What decisions could he have made which might have changed the result of the war?

3 Read carefully the events after 1646.
  • What was Charles' attitude after 1646?
  • Did this make his trial and execution inevitable?

EXTENSION ACTIVITY

1 'A sad eyed martyr or a cunning conspirator who would never admit defeat.' These are two extreme views of Charles.
  • What alternatives can you suggest which might fit the evidence in this unit?
  • Discuss these in a small group.

15. OLIVER CROMWELL

Targets

* To consider primary evidence about the Commonwealth period.
* To identify the problems facing Oliver Cromwell as ruler.

In 1649 Cromwell showed no mercy when he suppressed the Catholics in Ireland. At Drogheda the inhabitants were massacred.

The young Prince of Wales was recognised as Charles II by the Scottish Presbyterians. Cromwell defeated him at Worcester on September 3rd, 1651 but Charles escaped, hiding for a time, according to legend, in an oak tree.

The death of Charles I was followed by a Catholic uprising in Ireland and the threat of invasion by France and Spain. The government depended on the support of Oliver Cromwell's army. Using some primary sources we may be able to see how this Puritan general tried to bring peace and order to England before his death in 1658.

B

I forebade them to spare any that were in arms in the town, and, I think, that night they put to the sword about 2 000 men ... I am persuaded that this is a righteous judgment of God upon these barbarous wretches ... it will tend to prevent the effusion (shedding) of blood for the future ... God alone have all the glory.

Letter from Cromwell to the Speaker of the House of Commons, September 17, 1649.

C

The enemy hath had great loss: and certainly is scattered ... this hath been a very glorious mercy - and as stiff a contest, for four or five hours, as ever I have seen.

Cromwell to the Speaker, September 3, 1651.

By 1652 the Rump was very unpopular. Its members were corrupt and did nothing to reduce heavy taxes. On April 20th 1653 Cromwell acted.

D

(The General) brought in five or six files of musketeers ... pointing to the Speaker in his chair, he said ... 'Fetch him down' ... Then the General went to the table where the mace lay ... and said 'Take away these baubles.' So the soldiers took away the mace, and all the House went out.'

The Sydney Papers. A. Collins, 1746.

A

Oliver Cromwell. A painting from 1649.

 Do you think this is a realistic likeness of Cromwell? Give reasons for your answer.

A new constitution was drawn up, naming Cromwell as Lord Protector, ruling with a council and Parliament. The vote was given to landowners who were not Catholics or Anglicans.

> **E**
>
> 'Clause VI. ... laws shall not be altered, suspended ... or repealed, nor any new law made, nor any tax, charge or imposition laid upon the people, but by common consent in Parliament ...'
> Clause XVII. That the persons who shall be elected to serve in Parliament shall be such ... as are persons of known integrity, fearing God and of good conversation ...'
>
> *The Instrument of Government, 1653.*

Parliament, wanting more power, tried reducing the size of the army. 1655 saw Cromwell dissolve it, giving power to his generals. Each controlled one of 11 districts with the help of a regiment.

> **F**
>
> '... no unlawful assemblies be permitted ... laws against ... swearing and cursing, plays ... and profaning the Lord's Day ... be put in more effectual execution ... all gaming houses ... be ... sought out and suppressed within the cities of London and Westminster'
>
> *Instructions to the major generals, October 1655.*

G

Cromwell still stands guard outside Parliament today.

CORE ACTIVITIES

1 Read **B** carefully.
  - How did Cromwell justify the Drogheda massacre?

2 Look at both **B** and **C**.
  - What do they tell us about his character and beliefs?
  - Why do you think he dissolved Parliament in 1653 and 1655?
  - Why did Cromwell not try to rule permanently without Parliament?

3 Think about the oppressive measures taken by the generals.
  - Can you suggest reasons for these?

EXTENSION ACTIVITIES

1 Think carefully about Cromwell.
  - List his successes and failures after 1649.
  - What can you say about his difficulties at home and abroad?

2 Some historians argue that the events which followed Cromwell's death show that he was the only politician who could keep control of the country for Parliament.
  - Look at the evidence in this unit. What do you think?
  - Discuss your view with friends.

This military rule brought peace. A new Parliament met in 1656 and offered Cromwell the crown. He was tempted but knew that the army and independents would not agree.

Cromwell's foreign policy was more successful. In 1654 the English navy, commanded by Robert Blake, defeated the Dutch to control the English Channel. Spanish treasure fleets were captured and Jamaica became an English possession. The reputation of England as a military, naval and commercial power increased.

Following Cromwell's death, popular support for the return of the Stuarts grew as Parliament and the army struggled for control. Finally, George Monck, a general who believed the army should obey Parliament, marched on London and prepared the way for Charles II.

16. THE MERRY MONARCH

Targets

* To investigate the results of the Restoration.
* To consider how Charles's personality led to further arguments between Crown and Parliament.

The mood of the country in 1660 was very different from ten years earlier when the 20 year old Prince Charles had fled into exile.

The end of the harsh military rule of Cromwell and the Puritans' suppression of all forms of entertainment and enjoyment was bound to be expressed in a warm welcome for the new young king.

It was clear that he could not turn the clock back and forget the sacrifices of those who had tried to reduce the power of the Crown over the rich farmers and merchants who sat in Parliament.

If we look at his key decisions at the start of the reign we may see whether Charles showed that he was going to be more moderate than his father and avoid a new conflict.

Pardoning his Enemies
Only 50 Parliamentary leaders were punished for their part in the civil war, including his father's trial and death. Eleven of these were executed.

Land
The royalists returning from exile wanted their land back from Cromwell's supporters. Estates which had been confiscated were restored but those who had sold up could not regain their property and status in society. New families appeared among the landed aristocracy of the kingdom.

Religion
The Church of England ruled by bishops was restored. All MPs, town councillors and clergy had to be Anglicans. As a result the Puritans or 'non-conformists' were driven out of power in the Church and politics.

Finance
The army was paid off and disbanded, but Parliament refused to give Charles enough money to run the government or his own household, which included several mistresses.

Charles II.

Political Power
The House of Lords was restored with bishops and royalist peers. Charles could choose his advisers and decide when to call Parliament. But the MPs made sure that they controlled government through the purse strings and could discuss any issue on which the king spent the money it granted.

Here was a system in which neither the king nor Parliament had the upper hand. If they could agree all might be well.

Role of the individual

Charles showed a lot of common sense. He had an image which brought him popularity: handsome, witty, friendly, with an eye for the ladies. He was probably too lazy to seek more power for himself. However, he was unscrupulous and deceitful when it suited him, especially in defence of his family, including his Catholic younger brother, James.

Charles's foreign policy was dominated by his close friendship with Louis XIV of France. This absolute ruler had ambitions to dominate Europe with his vast army and wealth. Charles joined him in wars against the Dutch, who were England's major trading rivals. These cost Charles over £6 million. He also made a secret agreement with Louis to give Catholics freedom of worship. Parliament suspected this and passed the Test Act by which every office holder had to take Anglican communion. James, Duke of York, resigned as Lord High Admiral.

Titus Oates in the pillory. He was eventually exposed as a liar and punished.

The Popish Plot of 1678 showed how popular fear of a return to Catholicism had grown. The so called plot involved Charles's murder, the massacre of Protestants and James becoming king. It was 'revealed' to Sir Edmund Godfrey, a JP, by Titus Oates, a former priest who had changed his religion twice. When Godfrey was found murdered, Oates claimed the Papists were to blame. In a climate of near hysteria against Catholics, 35 men were executed for 'plotting'. Parliament wanted James excluded from the succession in favour of a Protestant. Two parties emerged, the courtiers or 'Tories', and the 'Whigs'.

Eventually Charles decided to try to rule without Parliament in 1681. Instead of losing popularity, the king appeared to be the guardian of law and order against the increasingly violent and extreme Whigs. When they plotted to murder Charles in 1683, the leaders were tried for treason or fled abroad. Two years later Charles died, having been received back into the Catholic Church. With plenty of royalists in Parliament and the law courts and a standing army, it seemed that the Crown had won.

CORE ACTIVITIES

1 Think carefully about the decisions Charles made in 1660.
   - Were they sensible and to his advantage or were they bound to lead to problems in the future?
   - How far did these decisions fit in with what we know about Charles' character and personality?

2 Think about Charles' foreign policy.
   - How similar was it to Cromwell's?
   - Why did it lead to difficulties at home?

EXTENSION ACTIVITY

1 The Crown was in a strong position when Charles died.
   - How far was Charles himself responsible for this?
   - Was this mainly the result of the mistakes made by his political opponents?
   - Discuss this in your small group and try to put together a summary of your conclusions on a large sheet for a class wall display.

17. THE PLAGUE & FIRE OF LONDON

Targets

* To consider contemporary sources on these events.
* To investigate how far such evidence shows the significance of these disasters.

Plagues were a regular occurrence in England during the Middle Ages and later. We have seen the awful effects of the Black Death in the mid-14th century. When this same bubonic plague returned in 1665 people still had few defences against it. With a population of over 300 000, London was ten times larger than any other city. Some parts were squalid, overcrowded, smelly and dirty slums. Black rats were common place and they carried fleas which in turn, carried the plague. Any infection spread quickly.

A

June 7th 1665. ... I did in Drury Lane see two or three houses marked with a red cross on the doors and 'Lord have mercy upon us' writ there ...

June 29th. By water to White Hall, where the Court full of wagons and the people ready to go out of town ...

July 20th. Walked to Redriffe ... There dying 1 089 of the plague this week.

August 10th. In great trouble to see the Bill (of Mortality) this week rise so high, to above 4 000 in all, and of them above 3 000 of the plague ...

August 31st. In the City died this week 7 496, and of them 6 102 of the plague. But it is feared that the true number is near 10 000; partly from the poor that cannot be taken notice of ...

September 7th. 8 252 dead in all, and of them 6 978 of the plague ...

September 20th. Lord ! What a sad time it is to see no boats upon the River; and grass grows all up and down White Hall court, and nobody but poor wretches in the streets!

The Diary of Samuel Pepys.

B

The Plague Doctor. The beak contained perfume. Bad air was thought to spread the infection.

C

Any house containing the plague to be sealed up for 40 days;
searchers to examine each corpse to establish cause of death;
public entertainments to cease;
dogs and cats to be caught and killed;
fires to be lit in the streets;
bodies to be buried after dark.

Extracts from special orders of the Lord Mayor of London.

Evidence

D — *Diseases and casualities this year.*

Abbortive and Stillborne	617	Executed	21	Palsie	30
Aged	1545	Flox and Smal Pox	655	Plague	68596
Ague and Feaver	5257	Found dead in streets, fields &c.	20	Plannet	6
Appoplex and Suddenly	116	French Pox	86	Plurisie	15
Bedrid	10	Frighted	23	Poysoned	1
Blalled	5	Gout and Sciatica	27	Quinsie	35
Bleeded	16	Grief	46	Rickets	557
Bloudy Flux, Scowring & Flux	185	Griping in the Guts	1288	Rising of the Lights	397
Burnt and Scalded	8	Hangd & made away themselves	7	Rupture	34
Calenture	3	Headmould shot & Mouldfallen	14	Scurvy	105
Cancer, Gangrene and Fistula	56	Jaundies	110	Shingles and Swine pox	2
Canker and Thrush	111	Impostume	227	Sores, Ulcers, broken and bruised	
Childbed	625	Kild by several accidents	46	Limbes	82
Chrisomes and Infants	1258	Kings Evill	86	Spleen	14
Cold and Cough	68	Leprosie	2	Spotted Feaver and Purples	1929
Collick and Winde	134	Lethargy	14	Stopping of the Stomack	332
Consumption and Tissick	4808	Livergrowne	20	Stone and Strangury	98
Convulsion and Mother	2036	Meagrom and Headach	12	Surfet	1251
Distracted	5	Measles	7	Teeth and Worms	2614
Dropsie and Timpany	1478	Murthered, and Shot	9	Vomiting	51
Drowned	50	Overlaid and Starved	45	VVen	1

Christened	Males	5114	Buried	Males	48569
	Females	4853		Females	48737
	In all	9967		In all	97306
				Of the Plague	68596

Increased in the Burials in the 130 Parishes and at the Pest-house this year   79009
Increased of the Plague in the 130 Parishes and at the Pest-house this year   68590

General Bill of Mortality for 1665. This provides a list of all the known causes of death in London in 1665.

 Can you spot any diseases from which we would not expect to die today?

The Plague subsided in the autumn but returned in 1666. On September 2nd another disaster struck the capital - The Great Fire.

After four days 13,500 houses, 89 churches and many other buildings had been destroyed but only six people lost their lives. With 80% of the city affected many Londoners found themselves penniless as well as homeless.

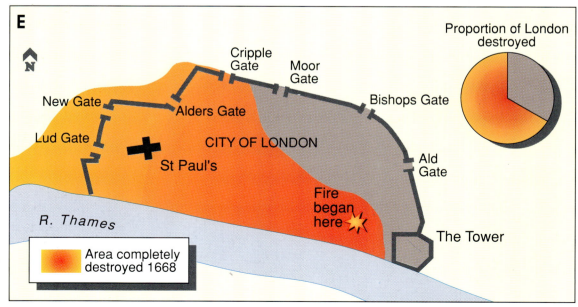

Sketch map of London after the Great Fire 1666.

Evidence

F

I shall give you ye best account I can of our late sad fire. It began at a Baker's house in Pudding Lane on Sunday morning about 2 or 3 of ye clock; and burnt down several houses but could not be quencht. It was a narrow place where engines could not play, and ye Lord Mayor did not think fit to pull down any further houses to prevent further spreading. About 10 of ye clock whilst we were at church there was a cry in the streets that the Dutch and French had fired ye city.

Edward Atkyns in a letter to his brother, 1666.

G

September 2nd. I down to the waterside and there saw a lamentable fire. Poor people staying in their houses as long as till the very fire touched them, and then running into boats; met my Lord Mayor in Canning Street, like a man spent, with a hankercher about his neck. He cried, like a fainting woman, 'Lord what can I do? People will not obey me. I have been pulling down houses but the fire overtakes us faster than we can do it.' Met with the King and Duke of York in their barge. Their order was only to pull down houses apace ...

Diary of Samuel Pepys, 1666.

H

September 7th. The people who now walked about the ruins, appeared like men in some dismal desert to which was added the stench that came from some poor creatures' bodies. The ground and air, smoke and fiery vapour continued so intense, my hair being almost singed. One might have seen two hundred thousand people laying along by their heaps of what they could save, yet not asking one penny for reliefe, which appeared to me a stranger sight than any I had yet beheld.

The Diary of John Evelyn, 1666.

CORE ACTIVITIES

1. Many precautions were taken against the plague.
   - Can you explain the reasons for these precautions?

2. Look at **B**.
   - Why did the plague doctor wear such clothes in summer?

3. Look at the figures given by Pepys in **A**.
   - According to these figures when was the plague at its worst?

4. Study the information on these pages.
   - What does it tell us about the effects of the plague on the normal life of the city?
   - What similarities can you find between the causes of both disasters?

5. Look at **F**, **G** and **H**.
   - What did the authorities try to do to stop the fire?
   - Why do you think it was not very effective?
   - Can you explain the last comment in the extract from John Evelyn's diary?

EXTENSION ACTIVITIES

1. What evidence do these sources provide about the feelings of people at the time?
   - In a small group discussion you could make a list of these and compare it with other groups.

2. Do people tend to exaggerate what they write or say about such disasters?
   - Can you think of any modern examples of this from the press or television?
   - Can you find examples of what might be exaggeration in the sources in this unit?
   - What does this mean for the reliability of the sources in this unit?

18. THE GLORIOUS REVOLUTION

Targets

* To investigate the causes of James II's downfall.
* To examine why the Revolution was called 'Glorious'.

James II succeeded to the throne in February 1685. This 51 year old Catholic found his main support among Anglican Tories.

In character he was more like his father than his brother. James believed he had a mission to restore the Catholic faith in England. He was prepared to fight a civil war to achieve it.

James II and his first wife, Anne Hyde.

Rebellions in the West

In the spring of 1685, the Duke of Monmouth, one of Charles II's illegitimate offspring, landed in Dorset to claim the throne on behalf of Protestants. His poorly equipped force was cut to pieces in the marshes of Sedgemoor in Somerset during the early hours of July 6th. Monmouth was beheaded; 300 of his followers were publicly hanged during Judge Jeffreys' Bloody Assizes across the West Country. Another 800 were sent in chains to the Caribbean.

Some Protestants saw this harsh suppression as a bad omen for their future. Would Parliament be strong enough to resist the return of Catholicism?
James kept his army of 13 000 men intact, appointing Catholic officers. Titus Oates was dragged through the streets of London and lashed. Across the Channel, Louis XIV was persecuting French Huguenots (Protestants). Many fled to England for refuge.

Causation and Motivation

Parliament refused to agree to James' demand to repeal the Test Act which stated that only Anglicans could hold military or government posts. The king ignored this and appointed Catholics as his advisers, judges and university chancellors. Monasteries were opened and a new ecclesiastical court was set up to expel Anglican clergy who criticised the king.

In 1687, James dissolved Parliament, saying his main aim was 'the advancement of the Catholic religion'. The next in line to the throne was his Protestant daughter, Mary, wife of the Dutch ruler, William of Orange. It appeared that in the end, James' hope of bringing England back to the Catholic faith would fail. But in June 1688 his second wife gave birth to a son. This seemed so convenient it was suggested that the baby had been smuggled into the palace in a warming pan.

B

A playing card.

 What clues does this contain about the doubts surrounding this birth?

Six English nobles and the Bishop of London invited William to come to England to investigate the new heir's legitimacy and James' attempts to rig the elections for Parliament. On November 5th, the Dutchman landed at Torbay in Devon. Instead of marching quickly to face the invader, James hesitated. William began a slow progress towards London as the king's support melted away. His most trusted general, John Churchill, and his younger daughter, Anne, both deserted him.

William did not want James to become a martyr. He allowed him to escape to France with his wife and baby son. The Glorious Revolution was achieved with little bloodshed or difficulty; William and Mary found themselves joint rulers of England as well as the Netherlands.

CORE ACTIVITIES

1 Below are four possible reasons for James losing his crown. Read them carefully.
   - James was too impatient to bring back the Catholic religion.
   - He believed that when he became king most of his subjects would become Catholics out of loyalty to him.
   - James could have defeated William as easily as Monmouth if he had acted decisively.
   - According to Barnet, a contemporary historian, James 'had no true judgement' and believed all who opposed him 'were rebels in their hearts'.
   - Discuss each of the reasons above and say which you agree with.

2 William sent troops to help James to crush Monmouth's rebellion.
   - Why should he have done this?
   - Why did he choose to land in the same part of the country as Monmouth?

EXTENSION ACTIVITY

1 ● Which of these groups would have seen William's invasion as a Glorious Revolution?
   - Catholics
   - Anglicans
   - Non-conformist Protestants, i.e. who were not members of the Church of England
   - rich landowners in Parliament
  ● Explain your answer.
  ● Was it a revolution or an attempt to stop change in religion and politics?

19. WILLIAM AND MARY

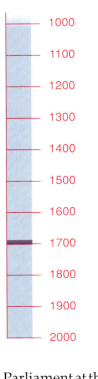

Targets

* To examine the political settlement after the Glorious Revolution.
* To investigate how far it ended the struggle for power between the Crown and Parliament.

William of Orange gained power peacefully in 1688. He was hailed as the 'Great Deliverer' who had saved England from a return to the Catholic religion and personal rule by the king without consulting Parliament.

Today the leader of the largest party in the House of Commons becomes Prime Minister and head of government. The Crown has little power compared with Parliament.

Unlike many other countries, Britain does not have a written constitution. The agreements made between William III and his Parliament at this time provide some important statements about the way we have been governed ever since. These agreements were set out in the Bill of Rights.

An oil painting of William III.

1689: The Bill of Rights

A special Convention met for three weeks to draw up this agreement between the new king and his leading subjects. The main points were:

▼ the Crown could only be inherited by a Protestant;
▼ Parliament should meet frequently and MPs should have freedom of speech;
▼ no taxes could be imposed without the agreement of Parliament;
▼ the king could not have a standing army during peacetime.

Parliament

Parliament moved on to pass other laws which laid down the foundations for the future:

▼ the king had to call a Parliament every three years;
▼ he was given an annual sum to live on called the Civil List;
▼ any extra money had to be voted by Parliament which checked the royal accounts and in effect controlled what taxes were spent on;
▼ freedom of worship was given to everyone who accepted most of the beliefs of the Anglican Church but Catholics and extreme Protestants were barred from public life;
▼ press censorship was ended.

Causation

The king still had some power; he commanded the army and navy, chose his ministers and decided foreign policy. In practice Parliament was now more powerful. William ruled by its consent, not divine right. The wealthy nobles, landowners and merchants who had invited him to come to England now formed a ruling class. How this might affect the majority of the people remained to be seen.

A contemporary painting of Mary II, wife of William of Orange.

The system of government was similar to the ideas of John Locke, a Whig who had fled to exile in Holland during the previous reign. In his 'Treatises of Government' he claimed that men were born free and equal. Governments are necessary to protect the liberty and property of the people. In his coronation oath the king promised to uphold these. Charles I had broken his contract with his subjects and had to be deposed as a result. This view of a social contract (agreement) between the ruler and property owners suited the Whigs whose interests had triumphed in the settlement of 1689.

William had to fight to hold on to his new crown. The Dutch were already at war with Louis XIV of France in 1688. James II gained French support and landed in Ireland where he could find plenty of loyal Catholics. William won a major victory in 1690 at the Battle of the Boyne. Although James managed to escape to France, Ireland was brought under English control by William's leading general, John Churchill. However, the problem of a Protestant minority ruling a Catholic majority there remained.

CORE ACTIVITIES

1 Think about the end of William's and Mary's reign.
  - Make two lists, one for 'Crown' and one for 'Parliament', showing what each side gained in the settlement of their reign?
  - Which was most powerful by the end of William's reign: the Crown or Parliament? Try to give at least three reasons for your answer.

2 The king became increasingly dependent upon the rich.
  - Explain two ways in which the Bank of England showed this increased dependence.

3 William III is better remembered in Northern Ireland than in the rest of the United Kingdom today.
  - Why do you think this is?

4 Even today, the Queen has little real power compared with Parliament.
  - How far was the Glorious Revolution a crucial stage in bringing about this situation?

Causation

To pay for the war against France new taxes on land and windows were introduced. Windows were bricked up to reduce the owner's tax bill. In 1694 the Bank of England was set up to lend money to the government, raising over £1 million in less than two weeks, to provide a sum which would never be fully repaid but which gave the lenders a good rate of interest.

An Act of Parliament established another source of loans; the East India Company. It controlled the important centres of Bombay and Calcutta, its commercial success bringing growing profits to investors at home. Such finance companies set up by Parliament show its increasing control over the Crown. The English navy protected merchant ships trading with North America, the West Indies, India and the Far East. This wealth gave English landowners the ready money to support the Industrial Revolution of the next century. At the same time, many people were wage earners. This 'working class' owned no property but sold their labour to survive. The earliest population census, made in 1688 by Gregory King, showed that almost half of the 5.5 million English people were extremely poor.

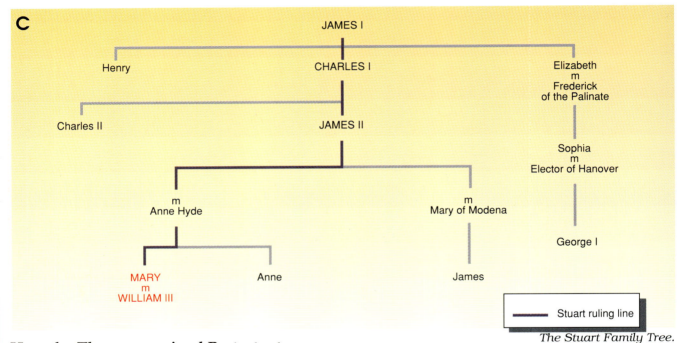

The Stuart Family Tree.

How the Throne remained Protestant

In March 1702, William III died, and his sister-in-law, Anne, became queen. She was married to Prince George of Denmark. They had had sixteen children but none of them survived into adulthood. She was a rather overweight and homely person who enjoyed the gossip of court rather than the detail of government. As a result, influence passed to the rival political parties: the Whigs and the Tories.

Her reign is remembered for a long war against Louis XIV, in which Britain was the ally of the Hapsburg Empire and the Netherlands, and for the political union with Scotland which was achieved in 1707.

When Anne died in 1714, the strongest claimant was James II's son, James, who had been brought up in France as a Catholic. Some Tories hoped that he would turn Protestant and become king. Instead, the throne passed to a distant cousin, George, the Elector of Hanover, in Germany. He was descended from Charles I's sister, Elizabeth, the young princess who had married a German Protestant prince in 1613. It was not a popular solution for many of the new king's subjects but the alternative of a Catholic monarch seemed like a worse choice.

EXTENSION ACTIVITY

1 William landed in England on November 5th 1688.
We celebrate another anniversary on that day.
- Draw up a list of reasons why the Gunpowder Plot rather than the Glorious Revolution is commemorated.

20. THE SLAVE TRADE

Targets

* To investigate the origins of Britain's slave trade.
* To consider its effects through primary sources.

Slavery formed part of most ancient civilisations. Portuguese traders brought slaves as well as gold and ivory from West Africa before 1500. The natives of South America and the Caribbean were put to work in the mines and plantations of Portuguese, Spanish, French and British colonies. However, the white men soon needed more labourers so the transatlantic trade in 'black cargo' began in 1518. During the next 350 years it has been calculated that over 9 million slaves were imported into America, nearly 2 million to British colonies. The ports of London, Liverpool and Bristol grew rich from the triangular trade which saw negroes crammed into ships on the 'Middle Passage'.

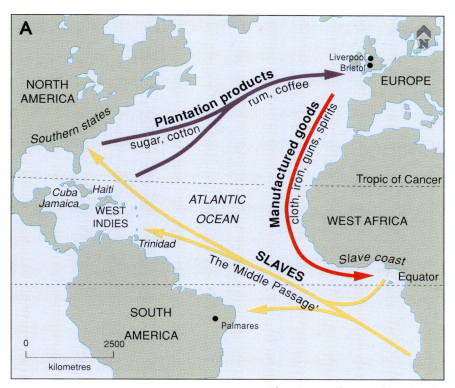

The Transatlantic slave trade.

Some first hand accounts from Africans have survived, mostly recorded in the 19th century. Some European writers also showed sympathy with the dreadful conditions faced by the slaves.

An 18th century plan of a slave ship. Each man had a space 2 x 0.3 metres; it was less for women and children.

C

'The village was surrounded by enemies, who attacked us with clubs, long wooden spears, and bows and arrows. After fighting for more than an hour, those who were not fortunate enough to run away were made prisoners ... we descended the river for three days, when we came in sight of what appeared to me the most wonderful object in the world ... a large ship at anchor ... I had never seen white people before and they appeared to me the ugliest creatures in the world. The persons who brought us down the river received payment for us ... a keg of liquor and some yards of blue and red cotton cloth ... At the time we came into this ship, she was full of black people, who were all confined in a dark and low place, in irons ... About twenty persons were seized in our village at the time I was; and amongst these were the children so young that they were not able to walk ... The mothers ... had them in their arms when we were taken on board ... the men who fastened the irons on these mothers took the children out of their hands and threw them over the side of the ship ...two of the women leaped overboard after the children ... one ... was carried down by the weight of her irons before she could be rescued; but the other was taken up by some men in a boat and brought on board. This woman threw herself overboard one night when we were at sea ... at the end of two weeks the place in which we were confined was so full that no one could lie down ... the ship sailed down the river ... We had nothing to eat but yams, which were thrown amongst us at random ... More than one third of us died on the passage and when we arrived at Charleston I was not able to stand.'

A Narrative of the Life and Adventures of Charles Ball, A Black Man, 1854.

D

'The slaves were brought in one at a time and mounted upon the chair before the bidders who handled and inspected them with as little concern as if they had been examining cattle at Smithfield market. They turned them about, felt them, viewed their shape and their limbs, looked into their mouths, made them jump and throw out their arms, and subjected them to all the means of trial as if dealing with a horse.'

Account by an English visitor.

E

'It was very common ... for the slaves to be branded with the initial letter of their master's name, and a load of heavy iron hooks hung about their necks ... The iron muzzle, thumbscrews etc. ... were sometimes applied for the slightest faults. I have seen a negro beaten till some of his bones were broken for even letting a pot boil over. It is not surprising that usage like this should drive the poor creatures to despair and make them seek refuge in death ...'

Olaudah Equiano's Travels, 1789. He was a slave in the British West Indies in the mid-18th century.

Evidence

Some of us may find the attitudes of the white slave owners and traders difficult to understand. Here are some of their comments:

F

'I've purchased nine Negroe Slaves at St. Kitts and can assure you I was shock'd at the first appearance of human flesh expos'd for sale ... But surely God ordained 'em for the use and benefit of us; otherwise his Divine Will would have been made manifest by some particular sign ...'

John Pinney, a sugar plantation owner.

The badge of the Abolitionists (anti-slavery campaigners).

 Why did John Pinney think it was alright to buy and use slaves?

The crest of John Hawkins, the Tudor seaman.

I

'Almighty God hath been pleased to make you slaves here, and give you nothing but labour and poverty in this world, which you are obliged to submit to as it is His will that it should be so. Your bodies, you know, are not your own; they are at the disposal of those who you belong to.'

Sermon by the Bishop of Virginia to some slaves.

Britain's involvement in the slave trade ended in 1807 after a long campaign by Christian humanitarians such as William Wilberforce and Granville Sharp. Slavery itself was abolished in the 1830s in British colonies.

CORE ACTIVITIES

1 Look at the information in this unit
- Why did the slave trade develop between West Africa and the New World?

2 Look at **G** and **H**. There is a gap of 200 years between them.
- Can you explain the purpose of each?
- If these experiences of slaves are typical, why did the Africans not revolt against such cruelty?
- Why did the slave ship owners allow such bad conditions on board if they wanted to make a profit from selling healthy slaves at the end of the voyage?

EXTENSION ACTIVITY

1 Think about the attitudes of white people in this period towards slavery.
- How many different reasons can you find for its justification which might have been offered by British merchants and plantation owners?

21. GEORGIAN LONDON

Targets

* To consider the appearance and character of the city in the early 18th century.
* To compare and contrast this with city life today.

We give the name 'Georgian' to the period from 1714 to 1830 when there were four King Georges in succession on the throne. Since the Great Fire of London in 1666, brick or stone buildings had replaced many of the old timber-framed houses.

The event itself was marked by a Monument, 61 metres high, on the spot where the fire began.

A visitor to London would have been impressed by the hustle and bustle of the great city in 1750 like today. The streets were still mainly cobbled so there was a perpetual clatter of horseshoes and coach wheels in the busiest areas. In the fashionable areas hackney coaches, four wheeled carriages and sedan chairs were the most familiar transport for the well off. Elegant facades, town houses with imposing doorways flanked by pillars, high sash windows and an overall appearance of balance and symmetry were changing the face of the old city. This style of architecture, which was influenced by links with Holland, grew throughout the 17th and 18th centuries.

A Georgian street scene.

? *Describe everything you can see in this scene in detail to a friend.*

The idea of elegance was also apparent in the costly clothes of the wealthy. Wigs remained in fashion; gentlemen wore three cornered hats and knee breeches to display a fine calf. Ladies in all classes wore long gowns; the rich preferred silks or Indian cotton.

The pleasant squares with gardens and parks brought a much lighter atmosphere to the wealthier areas west of the City. There were theatres, small shops, coffee houses and tree lined promenades. The main shopping streets had smooth pavements, and were cleaned daily. Traders called out their wares all day long; pedlars sold food and flowers from baskets and handcarts. The lack of drainage and abundance of horse manure brought odours which were familiar to everyone and could be offset by a posy or perfumed handkerchief.

Viewpoints

Georgian town house.

The atmosphere of Georgian London can also be seen in its plays. The leading actor, David Garrick, was also the manager of Drury Lane Theatre. Actors usually had to work hard to keep their audiences' attention. Cat calling and even pelting the stage with rubbish were fairly common. Sometimes the high spirits sparked off scenes more familiar in a Wild West saloon than a theatre.

The rate of London's expansion was remarkable. The dock system could not cope with the large number of ships bringing goods from all over the world. A second bridge was built at Westminster to relieve the pressure on London Bridge. The merchants and councillors of the city had considerable influence on the government politically and financially.

CORE ACTIVITY

1 In a small group discuss the sights and sounds of a walk through London in this period.
- What would interest you most?
- Prepare a short account of this 'visit' for another member of the group to read.

Of course there was a seamier side. Many slums remained. There was little sanitation, the streets and alleys filled with rubbish and whole families lived in single rooms with little light or hygiene. Disease and crime were everyday realities. Only one child in four born in London reached the age of five in this period. Many streets were unsafe after dark. The constable with his few watchmen were not trained as regular policemen. Visitors noticed mobs who might insult or even rob the solitary pedestrian. The laws against rioting and crime generally were severe; nearly 200 offences carried the death penalty. This offered the frequent spectacle of a public hanging as a popular form of entertainment on a par with visiting Bedlam, the asylum where lunatics could be viewed for a penny.

Alongside violence and crime went drunkenness. One visitor noted that everyone drank beer rather than water. Gin was sold by all kinds of traders. It was cheap but even so many poor people stole in order to forget their worries in a drunken stupor. Its evil effects were vividly portrayed by the cartoonist Hogarth.

Gin Lane.

EXTENSION ACTIVITY

1 Think about life in a large city like London in the early 18th century and today.
- What are the main points of similarity and difference between them?
- Make a list of these and compare it with the rest of the group.

22. SIR ROBERT WALPOLE

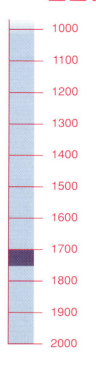

Targets

* To investigate the career of a political leader in Britain in the early 18th century.
* To draw conclusions about the system of government under George I and George II.

From 1721 until 1742, Sir Robert Walpole led a powerful group of politicians who controlled Parliament and kept the support of the king. Although he disliked the title, he was in effect 'prime minister'. How did he succeed in holding on to this leading position for so long? You may find some answers in these extracts about his career.

A portrait of Walpole.

? What does this tell us about his appearance and the fashions of his day?

Robert Walpole was the son of a landowner who controlled a parliamentary seat in Norfolk. He enjoyed hunting, eating and drinking; often he would crunch an apple during debates in the House of Commons. His large tubby body and plain speaking pleased most MPs who shared his farming background.

The king remained the most powerful figure in politics. He could choose and dismiss his ministers, create new lords, hand out offices which brought rich rewards, and call Parliament. The House of Lords was full of wealthy landowners who controlled many seats in the Commons through their influence. However, the lower house had control over the annual revenue. Unlike his predecessors who were peers, Walpole could provide personal management of the Commons to carry out the king's wishes quickly.

George II and Queen Caroline

In 1727 Walpole had to gain the trust of a new monarch. He soon realised that it was George's wife who had the greater intelligence and political understanding. His tactic was described by another politician: 'Sir Robert communicated the scheme secretly to the Queen, she insinuated it to the King, and the King proposed it to Sir Robert as an act of his own ingenuity'.

CORE ACTIVITY

1 Using all the evidence from this unit, discuss in a small group:
- How Robert Walpole held on to power as the chief minister?
- What he achieved in his period of office?

Role of the Individual

Economic Policy

Before 1750 manufacturing industry was not as important as farming in the country's economy. Woollen textiles were growing in some areas like East Anglia and West Yorkshire. Walpole tried to reduce dependence on imported goods such as timber and hemp for the navy. He introduced Navigation Acts to ensure that all goods were carried in British ships. Merchants were growing rich in peacetime, especially from the sugar, slave and tobacco trade with the British colonies of North America and the West Indies. Smuggling was a serious problem. Walpole tried to improve the collection of taxes and customs duties. He did not have any general plan and he was strongly criticised by London bankers and merchants who wanted the government to defend their trading companies against French rivals in America and India.

Walpole's mansion at Houghton Hall.

What historians have said about Walpole

- ▼ Walpole showed that every government needed a strong leader in the Commons who could explain policies and win support. He kept a tight grip on financial matters; afterwards every successful chief minister followed his example of becoming First Lord of the Treasury. He set the pattern for others.
- ▼ He was not like a modern prime minister. He did nothing to develop the Cabinet system of government. His success was due to the strength of his personality in keeping the trust of the king and support in the Commons. He did not leave a model for the future.
- ▼ He clung to peace and held back those trading adventurers who could win and exploit the wealth of distant lands. His instinct was to keep hold of what he had and not take risks. His skill was in manipulating men, not making policy. He lacked the vision to see that England's destiny lay in seizing every opportunity to expand politically and commercially.

Foreign Policy

Britain had fallen heavily into debt following long wars against France. Walpole succeeded in avoiding major conflicts until 1739. Then increasing disputes between British merchants and the Spanish government in South America led to war. A year later Walpole had to give in to the king's demand for help to be sent to Maria Theresa whose claim to the Austrian throne was being challenged. As a war minister Walpole failed. When his support in the Commons dwindled he resigned in 1742.

EXTENSION ACTIVITY

1 Take each of the three views of historians.
  ● Which one seems to be most justified by the evidence in this unit?

23. BONNIE PRINCE CHARLIE

Targets

* To investigate the causes of the Rebellion of 1745.
* To consider how close to success the Young Pretender came.

Since 1603 Scotland had retained its own Parliament and Royal Council. The majority of Scots accepted William III as king when he recognised their Presbyterian Church. In Glencoe the MacDonalds, the leading clan to support James II, were massacred by the Campbells. Scottish merchants were angry that the Navigation Acts did not cover their ships and in effect barred them from sharing in the growth of English overseas trade. When they threatened to choose their own king the two countries were united by the Act of Union in 1707. Scotland lost its Parliament but gained free trade with England and kept its own laws and Church.

The Young Pretender

Charles Edward Stuart, the grandson of James II, was brought up in Rome. In August 1745, he landed in the north of Scotland and won the support of the MacDonald clan. With George II and the main English army fighting the French on the continent Charles was able to march to Edinburgh. At Holyrood Palace the 25 year old prince set up his court and urged all Scots to join his cause. In London, ministers quarrelled among themselves but resisted the idea of recalling the army from abroad. Charles marched into England with an army of 5 000 in November.

Charles Edward Stuart.

Carlisle and Manchester were easily captured but no English joined the invaders. Charles knew it was only a matter of time before he faced a strong royal army. However, he hoped that the French might seek the opportunity to invade England too, or at least send him fresh troops and arms. On December 4th he reached Derby; there was panic in London. By now George II had returned and the veteran troops of the Duke of Cumberland were heading north to attack the invaders.

Charles was persuaded to return to Scotland. His army began to dwindle away; when he faced Cumberland on the bleak moor of Culloden, near Inverness, on April 16th, 1746 his remaining Highlanders were half starved and exhausted. The English artillery and infantry killed 1 000 rebels; only 50 of Cumberland's men died. The fleeing Jacobites were cut down and the government tried to stamp out the clan system, banning the tartan kilt and disarming the Highlanders. Charles himself escaped from the battlefield and for five months he hid successfully, despite a reward of £30 000 for his capture. Disguised as a female, and with the help of Flora MacDonald, he sailed to the Isle of Skye and eventually reached France in September. His cause was lost but some echoes can still be heard in toasts drunk 'to the King over the water' and the Skye Boat Song.

Role of the Individual

B

A Judgment on the Rebellion.
'No Englishman of importance joined Charles ... The Highlands were remorselessly, and finally, conquered ... But Charles Edward had been their one moment of hope, and, as despair deepened, he became a heroic, almost legendary, character, comparable almost to King Arthur, for in myths defeated nations find consolation.'

J.H.Plumb, England in the Eighteenth Century (1950)

C

Burnt are our homes; exile and death scatter the loyal men.
Yet ere the sword cool in the sheath, Charlie will come again.
Speed, bonnie boat, like a bird on the wing,
'Onward' the sailors cry.
Carry the lad who is born to be king, over the sea to Skye.

Part of the Skye Boat Song.

An artist's impression of Prince Charles Edward at the time of his rebellion when he was 25 years old.

CORE ACTIVITIES

1 Look carefully at all the information in this unit:
  - What made it possible for Charles to launch such a serious rebellion in 1745?
  - Having reached Derby, what made him turn back without trying to attack the English capital, 130 miles away?

2 Look at **B** and **C**.
  - What ideas in **B** are supported by **C**?

EXTENSION ACTIVITY

1 What were the key decisions which Charles had to make during his rebellion?
  - If he had decided differently, could he have changed the course of events?
  - Discuss in a small group and share your conclusions with the rest of the class.

24. SCIENCE AND SUPERSTITION

1000
1100
1200
1300
1400
1500
1600
1700
1800
1900
2000

Targets

* To explain why people were resistant to new ideas and change.
* To identify what motivated scientists of the time.

I wonder how many of you read your Star Forecast in newspapers and magazines. Do you really believe what it predicts or is it just a bit of fun?

During the period of 1500 - 1750, how the stars influenced your life, which is called ASTROLOGY, was extremely important and believed by everyone. People were also very interested in ASTRONOMY, which is the scientific study of the stars and planets.

By 1500 people were beginning to find out more about the world in which they lived. New ideas were being discussed. In 1543, Copernicus, a Polish astronomer, published his discovery that the earth and planets revolve around the sun. He had known this for some time, but because the Christian Church taught that the earth was the centre of the universe, he was afraid to make his findings public until he was an old man. Even the Italian scientist Galileo, who used the newly invented telescope to prove Copernicus was correct, was threatened with death if he did not admit he was wrong.

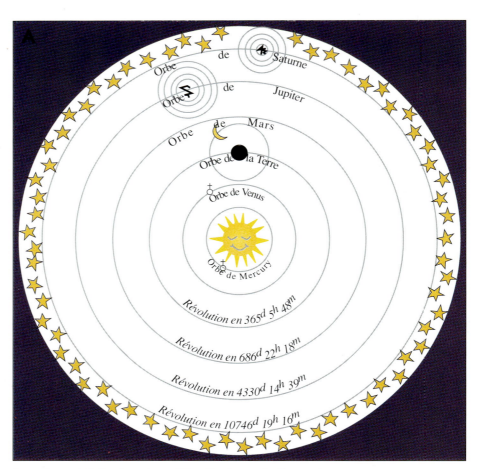

A modern artist's drawing of the Systeme de Copernic.

 Orbe de la Terre is the earth. How long does it take to travel around the sun? Why might this information have been important at the time?

58

Change and Motivation

Medicine

Progress in medicine at this time was very slow, mainly because superstitious ideas were still believed. For example, the touch of the king was thought to cure a disease called the 'king's evil' which affected the glands. Also if people fell ill and died it was often thought to be due to witchcraft. Many people were burned or hung as witches.

B

> First consider what planet causeth the disease. Garden rue is an herb of the Sun, and under Leo the seed taken in wine is an antidote against all dangerous medicines. English tobacco is found by good experience to expel worms from the stomach when taken by a pipe.
>
> *Nicholas Culpepper, The Complete Herbal, 1633.*

The Scientific Revolution

However, gradually more and more people wanted to find out about how the body worked and to answer questions about the earth and universe. From 1645 a group of mathematicians, scientists and scholars had been meeting to discuss new ideas. In 1662, Charles II granted them a charter and they became known as The Royal Society. Source **C** is a copy of the instructions which Charles included in his charter.

 What ideas does this source suggest that people had about the causes of disease?

C

> ... the Advancement of Natural Experimental Philosopy especially those parts of it which concern the Encrease (increase) of Commerce by the Addition of useful inventions tending to the Ease, Profit or Health of our Subjects ... to confer (discuss) about the hidden Causes of Things ... and to prove themselves real benefactors to Mankind.
>
> *Charles II from Charter granted to the Royal Society, 1662.*

 What do you think Charles hoped would be gained as a result of his charter to the Royal Society?

William Harvey 1578 - 1657:

One member of the Royal Society was a physician called William Harvey. In 1628 he discovered the circulation of the blood, a problem which had puzzled people for generations. Harvey carried out experiments and calculations and finally was able to publish a book which provided explanations and diagrams about the circulation.

D

> I have heard him say, that after his book of the Circulation of the Blood came out, he fell mightily in his practice (he lost many patients) and 'twas believed ... he was crack-brained.
>
> *Written by John Aubrey, a friend of William Harvey.*

 What do you think the expression 'crack-brained' might mean?

Change and Motivation

Other important members of the Royal Society

Robert Boyle 1627 - 1691: Published a book which became the foundation of modern chemistry.

Christopher Wren 1632 - 1723: Although best known as an architect, had many other skills and interests. He was a professor of astronomy at Oxford University, where he used mathematical principles to design buildings.

Robert Hooke 1635 - 1703: Professor of geometry, astronomer and designer of a microscope and marine barometer.

Edmund Halley 1656 - 1742: Published Isaac Newton's book *Principia Mathematica* and discovered the orbit of the comet known as 'Halley's comet'.

Isaac Newton 1642 - 1727: Isaac Newton was probably the most important scientist and member of the Royal Society in this period. After studying at Cambridge he spent many years conducting experiments about light and optics. He also worked on his theory of gravity; from this theory he was able to calculate the orbits of the planets. Eventually Newton's findings were published in a book called *Principia Mathematica* in 1686. Modern maths, physics and astronomy are based on Newton's book and findings.

Sir Isaac Newton painted during his lifetime.

 What sort of impression does this painting convey of Isaac Newton?

CORE ACTIVITIES

1 During the period 1500 - 1750 many people did not want to accept new ideas.
- Using the information in this unit make a list or design a diagram to show the ideas which people resisted.
- Use evidence to explain how you know that people resisted the change.
- Explain why you think people did not want to accept each new idea.
- Why you think people continued to investigate new ideas despite the fact that other people opposed them.

2 Using the information in this unit:
- Explain why you think so many new ideas were developed during the period 1600 - 1750.

EXTENSION ACTIVITIES

1 Choose any of the people mentioned in this unit and find out more about their work and discoveries. You could work in a small group and produce a Royal Society's who's who!

2 Working with a partner produce a radio programme or video about:
- Witches and witchcraft in the 17th century.
- Medical beliefs and developments 1500 - 1750.

25. THE FORMATION OF THE UK

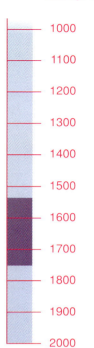

Targets

* To think about how the country was united.
* To investigate how far each nation remained separate.

During the period covered by this book, England took political control of the other three nations, Wales, Scotland and Ireland. However, they each kept some degree of independence.

Wales

The principality had been conquered by Edward I (1272-1307). In 1536 Henry VIII's Parliament passed an act which divided it into counties under the same system of law as England. For the first time Wales sent MPs to Westminster. Today Welsh nationalists still campaign for a separate parliament and government. Some government departments have Welsh sections such as Education.

Ireland

Religion has dominated the history of Ireland since Tudor times. There were long wars during the reign of Elizabeth I when the Protestant church found few supporters there. James I gave confiscated land in the northern province of Ulster to English and Scottish protestants. This remains fiercely loyal to the Church and Crown of England today. Of course the southern part of Ireland is no longer part of the United Kingdom and is the independent Republic of Ireland.

Scotland

Despite having the same monarch as England from 1603 it remained independent until 1707. As we have seen, the Act of Union meant that Scotland sent MPs to the House of Commons but many Scots, not only Catholic supporters of the Jacobites, resented being ruled from London. Today Scotland retains its own legal system and form of local government.

A

The Union Flag in 1707.

? *In what ways does this differ from the modern Union Jack?*

B

CORE ACTIVITY

1 The making of the United Kingdom can be seen as a process of England gaining control of the rest.
* Using other sections in this book and your own knowledge of the period from 1500 onwards, can you provide evidence of ways in which these other countries influenced England?
(CLUE TO SUCCESS: The Tudor and Stuart monarchs; religion; civil war)

INDEX

A

Anne, Queen	45
Armada	22 - 24

B

Ball, Charles	50
Bill (Declaration) of Rights	46
Blake, Robert	38
Boleyn, Anne	4, 11 - 13, 18
Boyle, Robert	60
Boyne, Battle of the	47
Buckingham, Duke of	33

C

Caroline, Queen	54
Catesby, Robert	29
Catherine of Aragon	7, 11 - 12, 17
Cecil, Robert	28 - 30
Cecil, William, Lord Burghley	18 - 19
Charles I	33 - 36, 47
Charles II	37 - 40, 43, 59
Churchill, John	45, 47
Copernicus	58
Cranmer, Thomas	12, 16 - 17
Cromwell, Oliver	35 - 39
Cromwell, Thomas	8, 12 - 14
Cumberland, Duke of	56

D

Dissolution of the Monastries	14 - 15
Drake, Sir Francis	4, 22 - 23, 27
Dudley, Robert, Earl of Leicester	18 - 19, 25

E

East India Company	48
Edward VI	16, 18, 62
Elizabeth I	4 - 5, 13, 16 - 25, 28, 31, 33, 61
Equiano, Olaudah	50

F

Fairfax, Sir Thomas	35 - 6
Fawkes, Guido	29
Field of the Cloth of Gold	11
Fisher, Bishop John	13

G

George I	52 - 4
George II	52, 54, 56
Giffard, George	15
Grey, Lady Jane	16
Gunpowder Plot	28 - 30

H

Hampton Court Palace	10 - 11
Halley, Edmund	60
Harvey, William	59
Hawkins, John	22 - 23, 51
Henry VIII	4 - 5, 7 -17, 26, 61
Henry, Prince	33
Hooke, Robert	60
Howard of Effingham	23
Hyde, Anne	44

J

James I	25, 28 - 30, 33, 61
James II	40, 44 - 45, 47, 56
Johnson, Dr. Samuel	6

K

Ket, Robert	16

L

Laud, Archbishop William	33 - 4
Locke, John	47
London	5 - 6, 11, 18, 25, 35 - 36, 38, 41 - 43, 49, 52 - 53, 55
Louis XIV	40, 44, 47
Luther, Martin	12

M

Marston Moor, Battle of	35
Mary Tudor	11, 16 - 20
Mary II	45, 47
Mary Queen of Scots	20 - 22, 28
Medina Sidonia, Duke of	22 - 24
Monmouth, Duke of	44 - 45
More, Sir Thomas	8, 13, 31
Mounteagle, Lord	29 - 30

N

Naseby, Battle of	36
Netherlands Revolt	20, 22
Newton, Sir Isaac	60
Norfolk, Duke of	20
Northumberland, Duke of	16, 18

O

Oates, Titus	40, 44

P

Parma, Duke of	21, 24
Pepys, Samuel	41, 43
Percy, Thomas	29
Philip II	17, 20 - 23
Pilgrimage of Grace	16
Pride's Purge	36

R

Raleigh, Sir Walter	4, 8
Reformation, English	12 - 13
Rupert, Prince	35 - 36

S

Shakespeare, William	4, 6, 26
Sharp, Granville	51
Somerset, Duke of	16
Stuart, Charles Edward	56 - 57

T

Tresham, Francis	29 - 30

W

Walpole, Sir Robert	54 - 55
Wilberforce, William	51
William III	45 - 48, 56
Wolsey, Cardinal Thomas	4, 10 - 11
Women, Role of	26
Worcester, Battle of	37
Wren, Sir Christopher	60
Wyatt, Sir Thomas	17

The Religious Settlement of 1559
(from page 19)
Elizabeth's solution to the religious problem was to choose the 'Via Media' (Middle Way). She made herself Head of the Church in England and adopted the Protestant Prayer Book of Edward V's reign. The Church was governed by bishops who were generally lenient towards Catholics. The clergy were able to wear vestments and keep their churches decorated with holy images.

TIMELINE

1500	
1509	Henry VIII becomes king and marries Catherine of Aragon.
1529	Wolsey dismissed after failing to obtain annulment of Henry's marriage. Reformation Parliament meets.
1533	Henry marries Anne Boleyn. Birth of Princess Elizabeth.
1534	Act of Supremacy makes Henry Head of the Church in England.
1536	Dissolution of the monasteries begins.
1540	Execution of Thomas Cromwell, Earl of Essex.
1547	Edward VI becomes king with his uncle as Protector.
1553	Brief reign of Jane Grey before Mary Tudor takes the throne.
1554	Mary Tudor marries Philip of Spain.
1558	Elizabeth becomes Queen.
1559	Elizabeth restores Protestant Church.
1568	Mary Queen of Scots flees to England.
1577–1580	Drake's voyage around the world.
1587	Execution of Mary Queen of Scots.
1588	Spanish Armada defeated.
1603	James VI of Scotland becomes king of England too.
1605	Gunpowder Plot.
1608	English and Scottish Protestants settle in Ulster.
1625	Charles I becomes king and marries Henrietta Maria.
1628	Assassination of the Duke of Buckingham.
1629	Charles' Eleven Years Personal Rule.
1640/1642	Charles tries to arrest the Five Members. Civil war breaks out.
1646	Charles surrenders to the Scots. Civil War ends.
1649	Execution of Charles I.
1651	Cromwell defeats Prince of Wales, Charles II at Worcester.
1653	Cromwell becomes Lord Protector.
1660	Charles II restored to the throne.
1665/1666	Plague and Fire of London.
1678	Popish Plot inspired by Titus Oates.
1685	Monmouth Rebellion against James II.
1688	William lands at Torbay and James flees into exile.
1689	Glorious Revolution completed with Bill of Rights.
1694	Bank of England founded.
1707	Act of Union with Scotland.
1714	Hanoverian period begins with accession of George I.
1721–1742	Robert Walpole's period as chief minister.
1745/1746	Rebellion of Bonnie Prince Charlie.
1750	